WHAT PEOPLE ARE SAYING ABOUT *POWER POINTS FOR SUCCESS...*

"Bob Harrison is one of the greatest teachers on finances that I have ever heard."

—Benny Hinn
Minister, Television Personality

"This book will impact your life. You will find yourself reading it over and over again."

—Peter Lowe
America's Premier Success Coordinator

"What you will get from Bob Harrison is very dynamic, and it is a great investment in yourself."

—Jim Money
Former President, Snelling Personnel International

"Bob Harrison has a way of pulling out of each article truths that will energize and empower you."

—John Mason
Author, An Enemy Called Average

"I truly enjoy what Bob Harrison has to say."

—Anne Beiler
Founder/CEO, Auntie Anne's Pretzels

"One sentence from Bob Harrison has produced years of increase in my life."

—Paul Brown
Director, Retail Logistics
Georgia-Pacific Corporation

"Bob Harrison is one of the most influential people in the world impacting achievers."

—Tim Storey
Founder, Hollywood Bible Study

"Bob Harrison is one of the finest teachers that I have ever heard."

—Myles Munroe
Author, Motivational Speaker, Business Consultant

BOB HARRISON

POWER POINTS
for
SUCCESS

WHITAKER
HOUSE

POWER POINTS FOR SUCCESS
Revised Edition
ISBN-13: 978-0-88368-406-1
ISBN-10: 0-88368-406-3
Printed in the United States of America
© 1997, 2005 by Bob Harrison

Harrison International Seminars
2109 East 69th Street, Tulsa, OK 74136
1-800-632-4653 • 918-496-3399
e-mail: Increase@increase.org
website: www.increase.org

1030 Hunt Valley Circle
New Kensington, PA 15068
website: www.whitakerhouse.com

Library of Congress Cataloging-in-Publication Data
Harrison, Bob, 1943–
Power points for success / Bob Harrison—Rev. ed.
p. cm.
Includes bibliographical references.
ISBN 0-88368-406-3 (alk. paper)
1. Success—Psychological aspects. 2. Success—Religious aspects—Christianity. I. Title.
BF637.S8H29 2004
158.1—dc22   2004018591

2 3 4 5 6 7 8 9 10 11 **w** 12 11 10 09 08 07 06 05

Acknowledgments

A picture of the late Dr. Norman Vincent Peale sits across from my writing table. Inscribed on the photograph are these words: "Dare to be what you want to be and *can* be." These words reveal the purpose of this book: to provide inspirational stories and innovative strategies to help you achieve greater success and happiness.

My best-selling teaching tapes and CDs about "increase thinking" have sold over a million copies worldwide. I am particularly appreciative of those friends and peers who challenged me to increase the influence of my life by adding books to my arsenal of teaching.

A heartfelt thanks goes to many of my friends and mentors, including: Peter Lowe, who is America's premier success seminar conductor, for constantly probing me to do greater things; Zig Ziglar, for all his input and motivation; Joe Ninowski, for introducing me to "The Book" that has most changed and impacted my life; Dexter Yager; Mark Victor Hansen; Myles Munroe; Tom Hopkins; Norman Schwarzkopf; Robert Schuller; Ralph Wilkerson; Bernie Dohrman; Brian Klemmer; and John Mason.

Also, I want to share my appreciation for the Premier Members of my "Increase Team" around the world, whose words, support, and changed lives have encouraged and motivated me more than they will ever know.

Working with Whitaker House has been an author's dream. Thanks to Bob Whitaker Jr. for all his input and enthusiasm for this project, as well as my editor Lois Puglisi, who has spent countless hours fine-tuning this manuscript.

In addition, a special note of thanks must go to my original copy editor, Jimmy Peacock, as well as to my executive assistants, Jodi Cook-Bailey and Kari Bloom, who assisted me so much with research and correspondence. I would also like to thank Sharon Cook, who contributed valuable ideas and has been such a positive influence on my life.

I want to acknowledge my mom and dad, Dr. Irvine and Edna Harrison, who are now deceased, but who provided me with a loving, stable home and a spiritual foundation that positively impacts me every day of my life.

A double portion of gratitude goes to my five children and their four spouses, who have been a blessing and inspiration to me beyond measure, as well as my late wife, Cindy, to whom I was married for thirty-seven years. Without her love, assistance, sacrifice, and commitment to excellence, most of what I am involved in would not have happened.

Contents

Preface

Within thirty days, your life could totally change as a result of learning and applying the various success strategies contained in this book.

Years ago, I was the operator of a large Southern California auto dealership. I had engineered one of the quickest sales turnarounds in Chrysler's history and was suddenly in demand as a speaker. Then the market crashed. For a season, it seemed as if people had stopped buying vehicles. To make matters worse, interest rates had skyrocketed, and I was paying flooring interest of almost 20 percent on my new-car inventory. In a short time, I was drowning in a sea of multimillion-dollar debt, exhausted from grabbing for "success straws." I would have given almost anything to have had the knowledge, wisdom, and strategies contained between the covers of this book. Instead, I had to personally begin a desperate search for answers—real answers—that could provide me with a needed lifeline to personal and financial victory.

During one of these crisis times, I was speaking in Detroit, Michigan. There, I met a millionaire industrialist who was my host for the weekend. This man had, in a few short years, accelerated his life so that he went from being a machine operator to owning nine corporations. He was also able to balance all the various aspects of his life extremely well and was a generous giver.

During our conversations, he reintroduced me to a book that he said had "the greatest 'success secrets' ever written." To my amazement, I discovered that he was talking about the Bible. I had always thought of the Bible mainly as a book of theology. Now a successful businessman was telling me that it was also a handbook of personal and financial principles for victorious living.

Over the next several months, I intensely studied this Book to discover its personal and financial victory secrets. I also began an intensive program of listening to tapes and reading about success and prosperity.

By combining my newly acquired biblical knowledge with my business acumen, I soon began to experience a total turnaround in every area of my life. I began to experience a supernatural increase in investments, real estate deals, and personal finances. I was living the life of an overcomer. I also experienced a spiritual renewal because many of my beliefs now had a solid foundation. My life took on a new vibrancy and meaning. I was a much more positive person. My values and priorities clarified, and fresh love rose up from within me for my wife and children. I was still busy and accomplishing great things, but now I was also at peace inside.

Over the next few years, I read hundreds of additional books, collected and organized thousands of quotes on various subjects, and interviewed scores of achievers from all walks of life to learn their success secrets.

Soon, business organizations, marketing groups, and churches across the globe began to ask me to come share my valuable knowledge. As people applied these strategies, many of them began to experience dramatic changes in their personal lives and businesses. I have received hundreds of remarkable testimonials and praise reports, such as the following:

A pastor in California told me that, after I shared principles of increase with his congregation, more than thirty-five members of his church had breakthroughs with their finances within twenty-four hours.

A networking marketing crown distributor called me and said excitedly, "This teaching has changed my life."

A businessman from the state of Washington testified, "In the last year, my income went from $25,000 a year to $140,000."

Another businessman, from Oklahoma, sent this extraordinary report: "Now, a few moths later, signs and miracles abound in my life. Since the middle of the year, my business has more than doubled. I have gotten very involved in my church. My marriage has never been happier; my wife and I are acting like two teenagers in love. I've been totally cured of cancer, and I've lost seventy-five pounds."

Plus, scores and scores of other reports too numerous to list.

Because of the dramatic changes that were taking place in people's lives, the door to the speaking arena flew open even wider for me. Soon I was speaking at the world's largest success seminars. I have traveled to all fifty states, been to over fifty countries, spoken to audiences of up to thirty thousand people, taught at five-thousand-dollar-a-person seminars, shared the stage with the world's most famous people, and appeared numerous times on radio talk shows and national television—all because the success secrets in this book work!

One day, I noticed an unusual thing was happening to me. As I read daily newspapers, I found myself automatically referring to a principle or strategy that I had learned and/or was teaching on. I began to incorporate some of these stories in my teachings, and I discovered that it helped people to understand and remember the principles.

Therefore, when I compiled this book, I decided to use a news story as a starting point or illustration for each featured life principle. These news stories will help you to remember the principles as they reveal humorous or practical applications of them.

In addition, some of the Power Points center around interesting or amusing incidents in my life or the lives of famous achievers. From these stories, you will learn how I, and others, personally used particular strategies and how you can activate them in your life situations.

At the conclusion of each feature, you are challenged as to how you might apply the principle to your life in a specific way. Let your imagination soar as you answer the questions, which are posed to jog your thinking and release the power of creativity into your life.

> **Power Point**
>
> "This is your time to translate intention into reality."
> —Bob Harrison

As a further assistance, a verse of Scripture is quoted to provide a biblical foundation for the success principle set forth.

Finally, let me share why I chose the title *Power Points for Success.* For this book, the word *power* can be defined as the basic energy needed to initiate and sustain action, enabling one to translate intention into reality. It is a quality without which people cannot change and leaders cannot lead. A point is defined as an exact spot, location, or time. I believe that the truths in this book can help you to create some personal "Power Points"—times when you become empowered to translate intention into reality.

I encourage you to activate the strategies, plans, and actions contained in the following pages so that you may enjoy maximum achievement, rekindled love, spiritual renewal, and/or enduring fulfillment.

Why settle for mere survival when you can live a life of power and significance? Determine to be all that you desire to be and all that God created you to be. Think of the life of excitement and fresh sense of purpose and fulfillment you have to look forward to!

Power Point Question

What is the best—and quickest—way that you can activate the Power Points of this book in your life?

"He...giveth strength and power unto his people."
—Psalm 68:35

Turtle falls from sky, hits man driving convertible, sends him to hospital

A Fort Lauderdale resident, who was leisurely driving his convertible with the top down, was hit in the head with an object. According to police, the object that hit him was probably an airborne turtle.

When I read this article, I wondered how a turtle could become airborne. Well, experts surmised that a seagull had apparently snatched a turtle from a nearby beach, begun its flight, then discovered that the turtle was too heavy to hold on to. As a result, it lost its grip on the turtle, which fell and hit the driver.

At home or on the job, many of us face a dilemma that is similar to what this bird encountered—attempting to do and/or hold on to too much. Many times, the weight of it all becomes more than we can handle, and we lose our grip on our priorities, our time, our health—even our relationships.

Noted speaker **Denis Waitley** tells of a time several years ago when he found himself in a state of overcommitment "with an overloaded calendar but not really building any lasting success....I had everything going for me...and nothing coming together. I had a house but not the home life. I had the family...but not the spiritual foundation so vital to relationships."[1]

If you feel overcommitted and under stress from trying to do too much, then read on.

GET-A-GRIP KEYS

Ruth Stafford Peale, the widow of **Norman Vincent Peale,** was a noted author and gifted lecturer. She and I shared the stage together at a success seminar in Little Rock, Arkansas, some years ago. The following are several keys to a balanced life that I learned from her.

1. KNOW YOUR PRIORITIES: Constantly remind yourself of what your personal priorities are. Make a list of what is really important to you in the long run and review it regularly.

2. TAKE THINGS AS THEY COME: Retrain your brain not to worry about the unknown. Be organized and plan ahead, but also learn to react to things as they come so that you will be better able to solve problems that arise.

3. MAKE TIME FOR RELAXATION: Don't think of relaxation just in terms of weekends, holidays, and vacations. Each day, carve out little niches of quiet time to reduce the pressure, clear your mind, and become empowered.

> **Power Point**
>
> "Carve out little niches of quiet time to reduce the pressure... and become empowered."
> —Ruth Stafford Peale

4. BRING GOD INTO YOUR SITUATIONS: Take time for meditation and prayer. If you seek God's guidance and receive His blessing of peace, you will be better able to handle any situation.[3]

In conclusion, do not let the extra weights of overcommitment and misplaced priorities cause you to lose your grip on what is really important in your life. In trying to hold on to and/or do too much, you—like the seagull in the above story—could risk losing something really valuable.

Power Point Question

Have you clearly defined what is and what is not important to you?

"The wisdom of the prudent is to understand his way."
—Proverbs 14:8

Wrong house raided

About a dozen armed police officers knocked down the front door of an elderly couple's home and held them at gunpoint while they searched the residence for drugs.

The police found no drugs in the home. Later, it was discovered that the lead officer had inadvertently written down the wrong address. Charging into the wrong place is the kind of decision that **Colin Powell** sought to avoid when dealing with other nations and that he seeks to avoid in life. Powell, America's former secretary of state, has held many leadership positions in which judicious decision-making has been essential. When he was chairman of the joint chiefs of staff, he was known for how carefully he prepared for battle. He would reportedly order satellite photos, send out scouting patrols, and collect all the intelligence available before deciding where—or whether—to attack.

POWELL'S DECISION-MAKING STRATEGY

General Powell, some friends, and I had dinner in Indianapolis immediately following a success seminar. I was impressed with how alert, articulate, and informed he was. However, he revealed something about his decision-making process that surprised me. He told me that if, "after collecting all the information that was available, a course of action was still uncertain—and if a decision did not have to be made—then I would wait. Time would often sort things out."

One of the most important characteristics of leaders and achievers is decisiveness: the ability to make tough decisions quickly. Sometimes, the delaying of decisions can create uncertainty and result in missed opportunities. On the other hand, what General Powell was saying was that there are times when deciding too quickly can lead to disastrous consequences.

I have learned this to be true through my own life experiences. If I do not have all the facts or do not feel an inner peace, unless a decision is required immediately, I normally delay the decision.

THE ADVANTAGES OF FLEXIBILITY

Here are some advantages of this strategy: Until I commit to a decision, I retain the ability to change, adjust, modify, or explore other options. In many cases, this flexibility has enabled me to discover better solutions, receive more favorable terms, avoid costly mistakes, and/or tremendously increase the impact of the right decision because of better timing.

> **Power Point**
>
> "If uncertain, do not make the decision unless you must."
> —Colin Powell

Rudolph Giuliani, the former mayor of New York City, uses the same decision-making strategy. He says, "Many are tempted to decide an issue simply to end the discomfort of indecision. However, the longer you take to make a decision, the more mature and well-reasoned it will be. I never make up my mind until I have to."[1]

Donald Trump also uses this approach in decision making. "I ask and I ask and I ask until I begin to get a gut feeling about it...and that is when I make my decision."[2]

Particularly when making big decisions, this decision-making strategy is worth considering. Remember—great leaders are not always the ones who make the quickest decisions, but the ones who make the right decisions.

Power Point Question

Are you losing flexibility and/or making costly mistakes by forcing yourself to make some decisions too soon?

"There is a way that seemeth right unto a man, but the end thereof are the ways of death."
—Proverbs 16:25

Bob Harrison   19

Plane loses door in flight

Minutes after takeoff, the commuter plane's cabin door blew off. Passengers clutched a flight attendant to keep her from being swept out of the open door.

The primary purpose of a door is to provide entrance and exit. However, if it opens at the wrong time—as happened on the Chicago flight—it can cause real problems. This is true not only on airliners, but also at the office and at home. Let me illustrate by explaining a problem that my friend **Dick Withnell** had with the open door to his office.

ARE "OPEN DOORS" YOUR PROBLEM?

Dick is a very successful Dodge dealer in the Northwest. Several years ago, I was visiting him at his dealership. During the course of our conversation, he mentioned to me that his business sales volume and income had greatly increased over the past few years. However, even though he was excited about the positive changes, he was actually feeling greater stress and having a more difficult time focusing on important tasks. He asked me for suggestions about what he could do.

As I observed how he was handling the flow of information and people that came to him, it soon became obvious to me what one of his main problems was the door to his office. It was located directly off a public hallway. Employees, customers, and solicitors could enter and leave through the door at will.

Although Dick's desire to be accessible was admirable, his "open-door policy" gave him no control over interruptions and distractions. Sometimes, his office seemed as busy as New York's Grand Central Station during rush hour. The constant traffic was robbing him of the privacy that is necessary for creative thinking, long-term planning, and meaningful conversation.

I advised him to remain "touchable" but to take control of interruptions. I also assured him that no one should be offended by this action if he remained accessible.

He activated my recommendation by moving his secretary's office next to his, cutting a door between the two, and giving her the open door adjacent to the hallway. He still remained accessible, but now she served as his gatekeeper, answering the phones and making first contact with customers and employees. His stress level went down, and his productivity went back up.

> **Power Point**
>
> "Lost time is never found again."
> —Benjamin Franklin

ADOPT A "SCREEN-DOOR POLICY"

If you want to be truly successful and effective, you must maintain mastery of your time. In particular, you must control interruptions. The strategy is this: Whenever possible, instead of having an open-door policy, adopt a "screen-door policy." Screen your calls and guests so that you can prioritize your responsibilities and maximize your time.

> **Power Point Question**

Who is in control of your "doors"—you or others?

"No one can come in to the inner court except with the king's permission."
—Esther 4:11 (author's paraphrase)

Giant sinkhole swallows home

A million-dollar home in a prestigious San Francisco neighborhood collapsed into a giant sinkhole. The hole was so big that a ten-story building could fit inside. Several days of torrential rains had collapsed a century-old sewer line, causing water to wash away the earth beneath the home's foundation.

Across the globe, many other homes are falling into sinkholes. However, these are emotional sinkholes caused by shattered marriages and broken dreams.

Like the home in the above story, many of these relationships appeared to be resting on solid ground. Then, suddenly, everything collapsed. This happened because, underneath the exterior trappings, over time, the very foundations of these relationships had eroded and washed away. Couples and entire families then suffered because of hurts, separation, and emotional trauma.

Several factors can cause a relationship to collapse. It might be the result of a lifestyle of continuous stress, which attacks a couple's intimacy and communication. Maybe it is wrong priorities brought on by self-absorption or the accumulation of material things. Perhaps it comes from continued verbal abuse. Or it could be from the boredom that sets in when old dreams and goals are attained and new ones are not created.

How can you reinforce the foundation of your significant relationship and help prevent a sinkhole? Here are some strategies that I have learned from a marriage of thirty-seven years and from interviewing couples who are experiencing long-term loving relationships.

RELATIONSHIP REINFORCEMENT STRATEGIES

1. COMMUNICATION: Learn to listen carefully, not just to the words being expressed, but also to the feelings behind the words.

2. AWARENESS: Become more aware of each other's needs and desires.

3. PLAYING TOGETHER: Have fun and share pleasurable times with each other. Schedule recreational activities that both of you enjoy.

4. ESCAPE: Periodically, break your normal schedules and routines of life. Take trips together to dream spots. Disappear for a long lunch or a weekend away together.

> **Power Point**
>
> "You are the one who gains when you strive to have a loving relationship."
> —Gary Smalley[3]

5. PRAISE: Nourish each other's egos and self-image through positive affirmations and sincere praise.

6. ROMANCE: Never stop dating. Practice being kind and caring to one another. Schedule quiet times for the two of you.

7. WORSHIP: Share common spiritual experiences. This will add depth, power, and intimacy to your relationship.

If you are not already doing so, activate these strategies. They will work when applied over a period of time with persistence and a loving attitude. You may not only avoid the sudden collapse of an important relationship, but you will also experience a life that is more exciting and fulfilling.

Best-selling author Gary Smalley states, "You may feel that it is impossible to change lifelong habits, but it is not. So try to change yours. As you make progress, you will gain confidence."[1] He continues, "But, don't expect miracles overnight. Anything of genuine worth takes time to perfect. As time passes, you will find yourself succeeding more frequently. Soon you will be right in the midst of the kind of marriage you never thought possible.[2]

Power Point Question

What can you do to strengthen the foundation of your loving relationship?

"The wise [person] builds [his or her] house."
—Proverbs 14:1 (NASB)

Giuliani starts investment firm

Hoping to become a big player on Wall Street, the former mayor of New York launches his own investment firm.

Since leaving the mayor's office at the end of 2001, **Rudolph Giuliani** has built a successful consulting business. He and his staff advise firms and governments on issues of security and leadership. Giuliani also has been a frequent speaker to corporate groups and at America's largest success seminars.

Giuliani's ability to lead was manifested by how he effectively handled all the events surrounding the crisis of September 11, 2001. It was also revealed by the positive changes that he instituted in New York City during his two terms as mayor, beginning in 1994.

One indication of the kind of changes that transpired during Giuliani's time as mayor was the reduction in crime. The number of homicides per year nosedived from 1,946 to 642—a reduction of 67 percent. Overall, crime was reduced by some 5,000 felonies per week.[1]

In the September 1990 issue of *Time* magazine, the feature article was entitled "The Rotting of the Big Apple." The story described New York City as a place with vanishing jobs, crumbling infrastructure, and soaring crime. It referred to the city as "the crime and welfare capital of America." Ten years later, the cover of *Time* featured New York City again. This time, the magazine called it "the safest large city in America."[2]

Giuliani says, "Leadership does not just happen. It can be learned, developed, and taught." He believes that there are many ways to lead, such as by example, by inspiring with stirring speeches, and/or by strength and consistency of character.[3]

Several friends and I dined and visited with Mayor Giuliani in Anaheim, California. One of his leadership characteristics, which really impressed me, was his concept of "starting small with success."

STARTING SMALL WITH SUCCESS

When tackling big problems, Giuliani would normally find and begin with some small thing that could be done quickly and noticeably.

For instance, when tackling the city's crime problem, he knew that it would take time to show significant results but that people needed to see some improvements soon. He decided to concentrate on two areas that could be changed relatively easily and that the public would notice. The first was attacking graffiti, which was a challenge for the whole city. He devised a program that quickly eliminated graffiti from subway cars, buses, and sanitation trucks. He then went after the "squeegee washers"—men who would rush up to vehicles stopped at traffic lights and tunnel entrances, spray the windshields, wipe them with a dirty rag or something, and then demand payment for their "services." These operators were notably aggressive, and many drivers felt intimidated by them. Giuliani had the police issue citations against them for jaywalking, and the washers were soon gone. New Yorkers loved it, and so did all the visitors who frequented the city.[4]

> Power Point
>
> "Small successes can change people's feelings and... boost morale."
> —Rudolph Giuliani

Giuliani stated, "Small successes can change people's feelings and can, in themselves, boost morale."

Power Point Question

What big task can you start by creating small successes?

"You have been faithful with a few things; I will put you in charge of many things."
—Matthew 25:21 (NIV)

Barry Bonds joins 700 club

When Barry Bonds hit his 700th home run, he became part of an exclusive club. He joined Hank Aaron and Babe Ruth as the greatest sluggers in baseball history.

I also had the opportunity to be a part of a 700 club. Only for me, it was an appearance on national television. I was a guest on a program called *The 700 Club,* hosted by **Pat Robertson.** Several months before I was on the show, I was able to begin a relationship with Pat. In large part, this happened because, before meeting him, I had learned how to use a sales strategy referred to as "creating rapport."

An Invisible Bond

I define *rapport* as "an invisible bond that is created between people." One key way to create rapport is to discover a common background, characteristic, or interest with another person or an audience. This process is referred to as "establishing commonality." When properly used, this technique can cause you to stand out from the pack.

For example, several years ago, I attended a VIP reception that preceded the Washington National Charity Banquet. Pat Robertson was one of the celebrities who was present. As a former presidential candidate and head of the Christian Broadcasting Network, he was being mobbed by friends, fans, and well-wishers.

By the evening's end, most of the people who were greeting him would be a happy blur in his memory. I desired to meet him and perhaps begin a relationship. How could I stand out in some way and create an encounter with him that would be memorable?

Remembering that my primary residence was in the zip code area that represented the second largest contribution base for his presidential bid, I decided to use commonality to create a bond between us. I boldly walked up to him, shook his hand, and stated, "Hi, Pat, my name is Bob Harrison. I live in zip code 74136."

As he contemplated my words, he paused and looked at me, confused. I said it again, "Zip code 74136." Then he realized what I was referring to. He grabbed my hand and burst into laughter. We had a good conversation. Since then, we have been together on different occasions, including my appearance on *The 700 Club.*

When I discovered and expressed a common interest, in one moment, I went from being an unknown to a person of importance.

Whenever this "drawing card" is discovered and used, you can increase recognition, favor, and sales. This is true in business, sports, and your personal life.

> **Power Point**
>
> "Rapport is the ultimate tool for producing results with people."
> —Anthony Robbins[1]

Use rapport to create invisible bonds that will cause people to remember you and want to be around you.

Power Point Question

How can you better make rapport a part of your personal arsenal?

"I have become all things to all men."
—1 Corinthians 9:22 (NKJV)

Teen riding waves after shark attack

Hawaii's number one amateur surfer remains unshaken and continues to surf following an attack by a 13-foot, 1,500-pound shark.

The shark that attacked thirteen-year-old **Bethany Hamilton** took a 17-inch-wide bite out of her surfboard as it also bit off her arm just below the shoulder. The teenager lost more than half her blood.

Despite the gravity of her injury, Bethany has refused to let this tragic incident get her down. Just ten weeks after the attack, she returned to competition at a National Scholastic Surfing Association meet and came in fifth place for her age category.[1] Since then, she has shared her inspiring story of overcoming a tragic loss on *Oprah, 20/20, Good Morning America, Entertainment Tonight,* and *Inside Edition.*[2]

Unexpected setbacks and misfortunes are a part of life and may suddenly appear, seemingly out of nowhere. This precious girl demonstrates the "bounce back" attitude that one must have in order to continue experiencing a life of meaning and fulfillment.

Many times, people can take a "victim" viewpoint in response to negative occurrences. This perspective is based on the belief, "Something is being done—or has been done—to me that has left me *permanently* wounded and powerless to overcome."

THE PRICE OF HAVING A VICTIM OUTLOOK

As my friend and superachiever mentor, **Brian Klemmer**, teaches, "There is a huge price to pay for living life as a victim. You may discover that your life is stalled out. You may find yourself unable to fulfill your true potential or achieve the things that matter most to you in life. Add to that a lack of respect from others, and it makes living for this victim viewpoint very costly."

So how can we avoid or come out of this negative approach to negative incidents? According to Brian, one strategy is this: "Look at the costs of being a victim, not only to you, but also to all the lives of those you touch." Determine that you are not going to let negative events become the defining moments of your life.

Another strategy is to take the approach that Bethany chose for herself. Focus on what you still have, not on what you have lost. As you continually place your attention and energies on what remains, soon fresh enthusiasm and joy will come forth from within and new dreams will emerge. For instance, Bethany's friends say that she "shows off what remains of her arm."[3]

Don't let accidents, past failures, or deep emotional hurts limit your life and stifle your future. Make a determination now to move beyond them and embrace the good that is awaiting you.

Power Point Question

How can you better respond to negative setbacks?

_____

"If anything is excellent or praiseworthy—think about such things."
—Philippians 4:8 (NIV)

Zig Ziglar receives award

Zig Ziglar has been named as recipient of the American Inspirations Award. The award is presented to a person whose faith in public life serves as an inspiration to all Americans.

Zig Ziglar is one of the world's best known sales trainers and motivational speakers. He has been recognized on three different occasions in the Congressional Record of the United States Congress for, among other things, "contributions made to elevating sales as a profession" and "his work with youth in the drug war."

Ziglar teaches that "success means doing the best we can with what we have. Success is in the doing, not the getting; in the trying, not the triumph. [It] is a personal standard, reaching for the highest that is in us, becoming all that we can be."[1]

Zig and I have shared the stage together from Honolulu to Miami and numerous cities in between. From our times together, here are some of—

ZIG ZIGLAR'S POWER POINTS

- You are what you are and where you are because of what goes in your mind.

- Regardless of your past, tomorrow is a clean slate.

- You can learn almost everything while driving in your vehicle.

- It is not what you have, but what you use, that makes the difference.

- If you do the things you ought to do when you ought to do them, the day will come when you can do the things you want to do when you want to do them.

- You were designed for accomplishment, engineered for success, and endowed with seeds of greatness.

- The greatest enemy of excellence is good.

- When you are tough on yourself, life is easier on you.

- For motivation to be permanent, one must have balance in one's life.

- Joy is the bonus you get when you put it all together.

- Where you start is not nearly as important as where you finish.

- Failure is a detour, not a dead-end street.

- If you don't like your output, then change your input.

Power Point Question

What input can you add to your life that will help you to achieve greater success?

_____

"A wise man will hear, and will increase learning."
—Proverbs 1:5

Government has eye that never sleeps

The Total Awareness Information Program at the Department of Defense may soon collect almost every type of public and private data on American citizens.

This program has been referred to as the "eye that never sleeps." A government agency might never sleep, but if you do not get enough rest, it could have serious negative effects—not only on your health, but also on your relationships and finances.

"THE SILENT CANCER"

T. D. Jakes calls fatigue "the silent cancer." Jakes is a nationally acclaimed author and megachurch pastor in Dallas, Texas. He often addresses this issue in his conferences and on his national television broadcasts. He teaches that "fatigue...robs [people] of creativity and secretly steals their energy and discernment. Tired people are...less careful. Even simple problems seem insurmountable. When fatigue robs people of their better judgment, they make permanent decisions based on the stress of temporary circumstances. Oftentimes these people are hard to work for and hard to love."[1]

Best-selling author **Laurie Beth Jones** concurs: "Leaders must be aware that their energy is subject to depletion and they must make guarding that energy reserve a priority."[2]

Bill Hybels, noted pastor and seminar speaker from the Chicago area, also warns of the danger of fatigue. He says, "Not only are physically run-down people short on energy, but they tend to be easily irritated, critical, defensive, and negative. It is hard for them to love others, and it is equally hard for others to love them."[3]

Richard Exley, who is a best-selling author and a friend of mine, says, "Don't deceive yourself. Rest is not optional...in Old Testament times, Sabbath-breakers were executed."[4]

Real estate mogul **Donald Trump** also believes in the need for rest. He says, "To be successful, it is not enough to have brains; you must have the energy. The true deal people sleep at night no matter what."[5]

Norvel Hayes, a multimillionaire investor and successful seminar speaker, told me something about rest twenty years ago that I have never forgotten. He said that often he could help people get out of depression and/or negativity just by getting them to take a break and rest. He exclaimed, "Tired people lean toward problems; rested people lean toward answers!"

If you have been pushing yourself or others too hard, why not stop the pace? Take a nap, go to bed early, enjoy a dinner without your cell phone, and/or escape—without your laptop—for a long weekend.

> Power Point
>
> "Fatigue robs people of their better judgment."
> —T. D. Jakes

Power Point Question

What can you do to break the cycle of fatigue and empower yourself?

"There remaineth therefore a rest to the people of God."
—Hebrews 4:9

New York cabbie sick after check bounces

A New York cabbie took a man all the way from New York to Michigan and back.

After the 3-day, 32-hour trip, the driver got a $2,000 check for the fare. Police reported that the check was no good and that the cab driver was sick in bed.

One does not need to be a cab driver to be "taken for a ride." I could not count all the counseling calls, e-mails, and prayer requests that I have received from salespeople and business owners who were having financial difficulties because of slow-paying or uncollectible accounts.

In most instances, I discovered that many of these people regularly provide goods and/or services to customers based solely upon a purchase order number, a verbal order, or a customer's promise to pay. Then, if the client fails to pay, they have to eat their losses. Not only that, but they also lose the profits they would have made by selling to someone else.

If you want to prevent this kind of scenario from happening to you, here are some helpful loss-prevention strategies.

LOSS-PREVENTION STRATEGIES

1. Reduce Your Exposure: On large projects or orders, require payment as the job progresses. Maybe collect one-third at inception, one-third at midpoint, and one-third at completion. If things go bad, having such a policy will greatly reduce your losses.

2. ESTABLISH CREDIT LIMITS: If you must extend credit, have pre-determined, written policies regarding how much credit you

are willing to extend. These policies could be based upon a customer's credit history, collateral, or the relationship you have with the client.

3. ELIMINATE ACCOUNTS RECEIVABLE: When possible, eliminate the risks by not having accounts receivable. Instead, accept credit or debit cards, subscribe to a check guarantee system, offer bank financing, or just say, "Cash only."

4. PRE-CHECK CREDIT: If you are going to extend credit, have some method of checking the person or company's credit in advance. Schedule times to periodically review credit.

> **Power Point**
>
> "Prevention is better than cure."
> —Erasmus[1]

5. INSPECT ACCOUNTS REGULARLY: Also, if you do carry accounts or extend credit, have a system in place for regular billing and follow-up procedures. Review these accounts at regular intervals.

6. PRAY ABOUT YOUR ACCOUNTS: Throughout its pages, the Bible gives examples of times when God gave understanding, wisdom, warning, and favor in the affairs of men.

Instituting the above policies will allow you to spend more of your time *making money,* not trying to collect it. Remember, what is important is not what you bill, but rather what you actually collect.

> **Power Point Question**

How can you better avoid and handle unexpected collection losses?

"Be thou diligent to know the state of thy flocks."
—Proverbs 27:23

Survival attitude helps downed pilot

An American pilot survived five days in enemy territory after bailing out of his jet, which had been split in two by a surface-to-air missile.

After ejecting out of his flaming plane and parachuting to the ground, **Captain Scott O'Grady** raced into the woods. Equipped with a survival pamphlet, radio, first-aid kit, distress flares, and a compass, he was able to survive for five days in hostile conditions by living on rainwater, wild plants, and bugs. Captain Grady "put to good use the lessons learned during 17 days of...training he had undertaken" at the Air Force's survival school.[1]

At this school, his instructors did not teach just survival skills, but also a survival *attitude*.

What is a survival attitude? It is a force inside people that enables them to rise up, bounce back, and even triumph in the face of negative circumstances. Normally, a survival attitude is not something that a person is born with; it is a learned behavior. It can be acquired from family or friends who have that attitude, it can be taught through actual training, or it can be developed by experiences in the marketplace of life.

DEVELOPING A SURVIVAL ATTITUDE

A great example of a person who developed this vital life skill through life experience is **Dexter Yager**. Dexter and his wife, Birdie, operate the largest network marketing organization in the world. I have been privileged to speak with them on several occasions. He likes to share how he developed the survival attitude when he was a child.

"While I was in the sixth grade, I wanted to make some extra money. There were several construction people working on a project in the area. There were no vending machines nearby, and the workers couldn't take off work to visit stores.

"I got the idea of buying soda pop for five cents a bottle, and then turning around and selling them for a dime. I could use the ice from my mother's refrigerator to keep the bottles cold.

"I began. Immediately, my business was a great success. Soon I was selling cases and cases of pop. I was earning more money than many adults.

Some vendors learned of my success and came in with their own ice and drinks. They were much bigger than me. I knew that if I wanted to keep my business, I had to fight back. That's what I did. I hired some kids to help me. We offered more drinks for the price and added different flavors so that we had a better selection. And on hot days, we made sure that we never ran out of ice!

"We won the battle. Our competition went away. For them, it was just another business, but to me, it was a dream come true."

A person begins to develop a survival attitude when he or she resists the urge to quit and instead fights back. Each action helps to form a habit, and habits create attitudes.

Power Point Question

What steps can you take to form the habit of resisting adversity?

―――――――

"Though I walk in the midst of trouble, you preserve [me]."
—Psalm 138:7 (NIV)

England's bobbies may discard helmets

The world famous image of Britain's bobbies in their distinctive helmets could soon be resigned to policing history.

Police chiefs are considering replacing the familiar 12-inch tall helmet with new head gear that looks like a bicycle helmet and can withstand a blow from a baseball bat. The decision to change the headgear of England's bobbies is not an easy one. The British love tradition. However, their police also have an appreciation for defensive armament.

Because England is an island country that has been attacked many times, the leadership of the country also has an appreciation for the defensive mind-set. This fact became quite evident to me during a lunchtime conversation that some friends and I had with Great Britain's former prime minister **Margaret Thatcher.**

A DEFENSIVE-PROTECTION MIND-SET

Lady Thatcher, Britain's first female prime minister, is a very charming, bright, and articulate woman. During her time in office, her nation began to rebound economically as state-owned companies and government-furnished rental homes were replaced with private ownership.

Also, during her tenure, Britain started to regain its tarnished reputation as a world power. Her defensive mind-set became clear to me when she said, "It is only with strong defenses that freedom can be maintained. Evil and conflict will always be with us, and so we must keep our defenses strong."

She went on to say, "For every offensive weapon that your enemy possesses, you must have a defensive counterpart, or you will eventually be defeated."

From my time with her, here are more of Lady Thatcher's insightful thoughts:

INSIGHTFUL THOUGHTS FROM MARGARET THATCHER

- STRENGTH: "A bully has no respect for a weakling. The only way to stop a bully is not to be weak."

- HOME: "It can be a base of operations, but it must also be a refuge."

- GOVERNMENT: "When a government allows its people and enterprises to flourish, then the country will flourish."

- ECONOMICS: "The way to recovery is through profits."

- FREEDOM: "You cannot have freedom without laws, rules, and responsibilities."

- OPPOSITION: "Sometimes you must be more concerned about the knives at your back than the guns in front of you."

- BATTLES: "You may have to fight a battle more than once to win it."

- PERSONAL ATTACKS: "People can be vicious. Don't pay too much attention to them or you will get a complex about yourself."

- ACHIEVING: "It is easy to begin a job, but a lot harder to see it through."

- SPIRITUALITY: "It is only in recognizing that people are spirit beings that individuals achieve importance and significance."

> **Power Point**
>
> "We must keep our defenses strong."
> —Lady Margaret Thatcher

Power Point Question

In what ways would increasing your defensive-protection mind-set change your decisions—economically, maritally, physically, spiritually?

"A wise man is strong."
—Proverbs 24:5

Resort town bans ties

Declaring that ties are detrimental to the resort image of the island, a city located on the Gulf of Mexico has approved a resolution banning them.

If you are tired of wearing ties, then South Padre Island, Texas, might be a place you want to be. And if you are weary of ending up tied in sports contests and/or in business, then better preparation might be your answer.

Experts agree that one of the best ways to improve the odds for positive outcomes is through increased preparation. A good example of how superior preparation opened the door of opportunity may be found in the life of **Mary Lou Retton.**

Mary Lou is as exciting and vibrant in person as she was in 1984 when, at the summer Olympic Games, she won five medals. Those who watched will never forget her perfect score of 10 in the final event of gymnastics competition. In doing so, she became the first American ever to win an individual gymnastics gold medal.

Today, Mary Lou is a popular seminar speaker. We visited backstage during a seminar in Tampa, Florida, where she was speaking. She told me that proper preparation is one of her secrets to success—in gymnastics, in the speaking arena, and in life. In fact, being prepared helped her get her start. She said, "I knew that I had to be the best in practice or I would not be the best in competition."

At the seminar, she shared how preparation also supplied her "big break": "One of my teammates was injured before an international meet. The coach turned to me and said, 'Retton, you're in.' Because I was ready for that moment, I was on the team from that day on."

Here are what some other superachievers have said about the importance of preparation.

Are You Ready?

"Talent alone will not make you a success. Neither will being at the right place at the right time, unless you are ready. The important question is, 'Are you ready?'"

—**Johnny Carson**[1]

"Games may be played in a stadium, but they are won or lost on the practice field."

—NFL head coach **Joe Gibbs**[2]

"Success occurs when opportunity meets preparation." —**Zig Ziglar**[3]

"The will to win is important, but what is more important is the will to prepare to win."

—College basketball head coach **Bobby Knight**[4]

> **Power Point**
>
> "I had to be the best in practice or I would not be the best in competition."
>
> —Mary Lou Retton

"Before everything else, getting ready is the secret of success."

—**Henry Ford**[6]

Power Point Question

How prepared are you for the position or dream that you desire?

"And he commanded them, saying: 'Behold, you shall lie in ambush against the city, behind the city. Do not go very far from the city, but all of you be ready.'"
—Joshua 8:4 NKJV

Collision with pole restores eyesight

The sudden restoration of a 63-year-old man's sight took place at a shopping mall when he accidentally walked into a pole. A childhood accident had caused him to lose his sight in one eye. The sudden jolt apparently dislodged the damaged lens that had been blocking his vision for years.

A pole also changed the course of **Jerome Edmondson's** life. It was not one that he walked into, however, but one that he found.

As a young teenager, Jerome determined that he was not going to live in poverty. When he told his grandmother that he wanted more from his life than that, she said, "Well, son, what are you going to do?" He replied, "I'm going to play basketball."

Jerome knew that his grandmother could not afford a basketball pole and hoop, so it seemed as if there was no way he could practice and achieve his desire.

He shares, "At about that same time, a storm blew through our little town. The high winds broke a big electricity pole and knocked it down. I immediately got a chain, wrapped it around the pole, and started dragging. It took me all day to get that pole home.

"I cut the pole in half with a handsaw. Then I dug a deep hole and tried to lift the pole. A farmer happened to drive by. When I shared my dream, he went and got his tractor and lifted the pole into place.

"Finding a sheet of plywood, I nailed a section of it to the pole for my backdrop. For a rim, I got an old bicycle wheel—took out the spokes—and hammered it onto the board.

"Now, I was on my way to fulfilling my dream. Every day, before and after school, I used my new basketball hoop to practice.

"When the day for seventh grade basketball tryouts came, I tried out. To my great disappointment, I did not make the team. Nevertheless, I was not about to throw away my dream. I went back home and continued to shoot more baskets.

"The following year, I tried out again. This time, I made the team. The next year, as a freshman, the coach asked me to play varsity on the high school team. Soon I was the best player on the team."[1]

The determination that Jerome learned as a young man set a pattern for his life. He went on to become America's first minority Denny's franchise owner and then the nation's first black A&W franchise owner. Today, he is the president of a restaurant company and speaks at seminars and conferences across the globe.

Jerome calls this process of holding on to your dream and walking it out step-by-step "tenacity." He shares, "Stay with your dream. The higher you reach, the greater your success."[2]

Power Point Question

Do you have a dream that you need to activate?

"What I am commanding you today is not too difficult for you or beyond your reach."
—Deuteronomy 30:11 (NIV)

American swimmers told not to spit in pool

The United States Olympic Committee gave American athletes some helpful etiquette strategies to use during the games. One instruction given to the swimming team was not to spit in an opponent's lane.

Officials gave this directive because they did not want the participants to do something that would intimidate other competitors or antagonize the fans.

Tamara Lowe had a different kind of problem by the pool one day. It happened in Hawaii where she and her husband, Peter, were scheduled to speak at one of my Increase Events. During a teaching session, she shared about the incident.

"The first day that Peter and I arrived in Maui, we went out to the pool. It was a lovely day—the sun was out and a breeze was lightly blowing. While I was watching my two beautiful boys, eight-year-old Zachary and three-year-old Blaze, play around the pool, I noticed Blaze toddling over close to the edge. When he got about one step away from the pool, he pulled down his trunks. Before I could react, he started to pee in the pool!

"Suddenly, people stopped talking and focused on what was happening. Some of them were shocked while others were offended. A few stared at me as if I could have prevented it.

"When my son came back over to me, I said to him, 'Blaze, honey, do not do that. If you need to go to the bathroom, come and tell Mommy.' He replied, 'And then you'll take me to the pool to go pee?' I said, 'No.'"

After telling the conference attendees about this episode, Tamara stated that the point to her sharing the story was this: "You can be at a luxury resort in Hawaii, your business can be going great, you can be making a lot of money, and you can feel like a king of the earth. However, in the middle of all that, someone might unexpectedly disrupt your life by 'peeing in your pool!'"

WEATHERING THE STORM

Tamara went on to share how we cannot always control what happens to us in life. Successful people are not the "chosen few" who do not experience negative occurrences. They just choose not let these negative experiences ruin their day—or their lives.

If you—or someone close to you—have had an experience that has caused embarrassment or negative feelings to set in, determine today not to let the power of any situation continue to cause hurt and inaction. As motivational speaker **Dennis Waitley** says, "Sometimes success in life comes not from having a good hand...but in playing a bad hand well."[1]

> Power Point
>
> "The real key to success [in life] is the ability to get back up."
> —General Norman Schwarzkopf, USA, Retired[2]

> **Power Point Question**
>
> *How will you respond to the storms of your life?*

"If thou faint in the day of adversity, thy strength is small."
—Proverbs 24:10

Man searches for his father

A U.S. sailor who fathered a child with a Chinese dancer disappeared from their lives over half a century ago. The child, now 56, is searching for his father.

There is an inherent longing in children to connect with their parents. This man is desperate to know who his father is and, if he is still living, to have a relationship with the parent who abandoned him.

There is a different kind of missing father. He is called an "Absentee Dad."

ABSENTEE DADS

Noted author and radio commentator **James Dobson** illustrates this problem with a story about a four-year-old who asks his playmate, "Where is your daddy? I never see him at your house." The other boy replies, "Oh, my dad doesn't live here; he just sleeps here."[1]

The son of a prominent national minister had a tearful reunion with his father in jail. The son repented of a rebellious lifestyle and drug abuse, saying, "I've spent my whole life trying to get your attention."

So how does one respond when career and family seem to be in conflict?

A key presidential advisor at the White House walked away from his job after his ten-year-old son wrote him the following note: "Baseball's not any fun when there is no one to applaud."

Professional basketball coach **Danny Ainge** abruptly resigned from his prestigious job, saying, "I wanted to make a statement to my family that they are more important than my career."[2]

Make Family a Priority

What these men did was right for them and their families, but success-oriented people do not need to become career-less in order to be good parents. However, they must make family a priority.

Lee Iacocca, former chairman of Chrysler Corporation, who literally kept the company from closing, made being a good parent a priority. When he was in town, he spent his evenings and Sundays at home with his family, saying, "My job takes up enough time without my having to shortchange my children."[3] He also stated, "Of all the jobs I've had in my life, no job has been more important to me than my job as a dad. I've always felt that when I die, if I can say I've done well by my family, then I've lived a full and good life."[4]

> **Power Point**
>
> "No job has been more important to me than my job as a dad."
> —Lee Iacocca

One strategy for being a more effective parent is to schedule family time the same way that you schedule your business appointments.

Another important strategy is this: When you are with your family members, don't just be there physically. Be there mentally and spiritually, as well. Let them have your attention and your emotions. Get involved in their dreams, their games, and their conversations.

As Iacocca states, "Other than family, what else is there that is really important? When it is all over, you are only as good as the sharing that you have done with those around you...especially your family."[5]

Power Point Question

What priority do you REALLY place on family?

"Fathers [and mothers]*, do not embitter your children,*
or they will become discouraged."
—Colossians 3:21 (NIV)

Doctors warned about exploding patients

A medical warning has been issued to doctors about people who might explode during certain kinds of surgery.

The above rare occurrence can take place if a certain anesthetic mixes with a patient's intestinal gases and accidentally is ignited by a spark from electrical surgical instruments.

I have had some experience with "exploding people." However, these individuals were not in surgery. They had an anger problem and seemingly could not control their outbursts.

DON'T ALLOW ANGER TO TAKE HOLD

Anger, in itself, is neither good nor bad. It is just an emotion. Whether it is a problem or not depends upon how and where the emotion is released. Problems occur when anger is released in an unacceptable manner. Unbridled outbursts can create barriers of fear and intimidation with others, resulting in the sowing of long-lasting hurts. They can also negatively affect the health and image of the individual concerned.

For instance, I remember watching news coverage years ago about the head football coach at a major university in the Midwest. He had an emotional outburst during which he allegedly punched a police officer. As a result, the coach was forced to resign from his prestigious job.

One strategy for dealing with anger is to find activities that allow you to "vent." Hitting a punching bag, throwing darts, swimming, taking a walk, or playing competitive sports can release pent-up emotions.

Another strategy is to document the times when outbursts occur. If there is a frequency of displays two to four hours after mealtimes, it is possible that low blood sugar levels might be a factor. If so, a change in diet might make a big difference.

An effective strategy for dealing with anger is taught by **Tim LaHaye**, who is a best-selling author and in-demand speaker. In his book *Anger Is a Choice* he states that "hurt and anger from past experiences can continue to affect us now." It could be very helpful to identify sources of hurt and anger from past and deal with those root issues.[1]

For example, author **Derek Prince** wrote about a young man whose life was changed by recognizing this truth. "[The man] had carried bitterness, resentment, anger, and rebellion against his father, who had been dead for years. He [drove] several hundred miles to the cemetery where his father was buried....He knelt [at his father's grave] and, for the next several hours, emptied out all his poisonous attitudes. He did not get up until he knew he had forgiven his father....His wife testifies today that she has a brand-new husband."[2]

LaHaye teaches that "releasing anger through emotional outbursts is a habit. Habits can be broken. A person need not remain a slave to that or any other habit."[3]

If you are dealing with an anger problem, make the effort to change. You will avoid damage to your self-image and needless hurts in your relationships.

> **Power Point**
>
> "Releasing anger through emotional outbursts is a habit."
> —Tim LaHaye

Power Point Question

In what constructive ways can you better deal with anger?

"He that ruleth his spirit [is better] *than he that taketh a city."*
—Proverbs 16:32

Star is rich and lonely

She makes millions of dollars per year and is known worldwide. However, in an interview, she reports that she is full of regrets and is lonely.

Money and fame cannot keep a person from feeling lonely. Even being around other people is not a guaranteed cure-all. Feelings of isolation and detachment can strike even in the middle of a crowd.

A feeling of loneliness not only can affect a person's attitude, relationships, and outlook on life, but it can also affect the person's physical health. A report issued by the National Institute of Health stated, "The most predictive risk factor for heart disease is loneliness."[1]

Catherine Marshall knows how painful and disabling this feeling can be. Before she became a best-selling author, she experienced a heart-rending bout with loneliness as a result of her husband's untimely death. She described it in this way: "During busy hours I could forget the pain of loneliness. Then some tiny thing...brought it all flooding back."[2]

I personally had to battle loneliness and a feeling of isolation after the unexpected death of my wife, Cindy. If you—or a friend—are feeling detached, sad, or lonely, here are some strategies to beat back loneliness.

STRATEGIES TO BEAT BACK LONELINESS

1. DEVELOP NEW DREAMS: Dreams give hope and bring a fresh spark to life. I remember a quote from an elderly triathlon runner who said, "No one is ever alone who has a dream."

2. GET IN MOTION: Find new things to achieve in. Don't fritter away your time; create, be somebody, do something.

3. CONTACT FRIENDS: Make a list of your loved ones, friends, and acquaintances. Make it a point to contact them regularly.

4. HELP OTHERS: No matter where you live or what your interests or skills may be, there are people who need your help. Show interest in their lives. It will bring joy to yours.

5. TAKE CARE OF YOUR HEALTH: Improper diet, low blood sugar, or other health issues can magnify negative feelings. Watch your diet and exercise regularly.

> **Power Point**
>
> "No troubles that life can bring need cast us adrift."
> —Catherine Marshall[4]

6. REST: Recharge your body. Tired people tend to respond negatively to situations. Rested people can normally cope better—emotionally and physically.

7. COUNT RIGHT: Focus on the good things that have happened and are happening in your life. Reinforce the positive by surrounding yourself, for a season, with pictures and mementos of your loved ones, family, and friends, as well as your dreams.

8. REMEMBER GOD: You are never really alone because God loves you. He is as near as your prayers. Catherine believes that this is the most important key. "Loneliness is a real wound—a gaping hole in the human spirit. It is God alone who can finally heal the brokenhearted."[3]

Power Point Question

Do you or someone you know need to implement the above strategies?

"He delivered them out of their distresses."
—Psalm 107:6

Swimmer loses trunks during race

The choppy surf created an unexpected problem for one of the competitors at the Pensacola Bay Swim. During the race, he lost his swim trunks.

After swimming in rough waters, **David Mayo** was embarrassed to discover that, while competing in the race, he had lost his trunks. He wouldn't climb aboard a rescue boat until he had some backup shorts.

The adversity that he had to deal with that day was nothing compared to what he had to overcome as a sixteen-year-old. One summer afternoon, while kayaking with family and friends in Idaho, David experienced a life-altering accident. He decided to climb some rock formations and, while doing so, slipped and fell fifty feet, landing backside on a boulder. Mayo told me of the accident, "At first, they did not think I was going to live."

While he was in the hospital, the doctors informed him that he had severed his spine and was paralyzed. Confined to a wheelchair, he lost all hope that he would ever be able to live a normal life again.

While we were having lunch one day, David explained to me that, several days after hearing the doctors' diagnosis, something happened that changed his attitude. An awareness came over him that he had been given a second chance at life. It was then that he determined that being in a wheelchair was not going to dim his love for life.

David began to participate in a wide variety of athletic endeavors. Soon, he was snowboarding and playing table tennis. Then he took up swimming, scuba diving, white-water rafting, hand cycling, and tennis. Since he particularly enjoyed tennis, David decided to hire a personal coach. Winning several tournaments, he has dazzled the competition. In fact, he was recently named "Florida Wheelchair Player of the Year."

David is now a successful businessman and happily married. He is living proof that adversity need not keep a person down.

"Success can be predicted by how one... responds to negative events," states **Dr. Paul Stoltz** in his book *Adversity Quotient*. "Those who are victimized by adversity become weaker. Those who respond to adversity as an opportunity—with a sense of purpose and a sense of control—actually may get stronger."[1]

> Power Point
>
> "Success can be predicted by how one responds to negative events."
> —Dr. Paul Stoltz

Dr. Albert Bandura, a Stanford psychologist and a leading researcher on self-efficacy, affirms this thinking: "People who have a belief in their... ability to meet challenges as they arise, bounce back from failures."[2]

Life can be hard. Negative events might unexpectedly happen. How you deal with them will determine your destiny. Determine to be like David Mayo, who says, "I am an eternal optimist who is always believing the best in things."[3]

Power Point Question

How can you better deal with unexpected adversity?

"If you falter in times of trouble, how small is your strength!"
—Proverbs 24:10 (NIV)

Fish removed from man's nose

After catching a 29-inch pike, a fisherman kissed it for a photograph. The fish suddenly lurched and grabbed the man's nose. It took an emergency room doctor to get it released.

My friend **Les Brown** says, "When you want something so badly that you refuse to give up or let go, you will probably get it."

Of all the speakers with whom I share the stage, probably none is more alive and energetic than Les. He has the incredible ability to transfer his enthusiasm and energy to his audience. Les believes that success-oriented people possess a powerful force that enables them to overcome obstacles and live out their dreams. He calls this force "hunger"!

Hunger is a powerful determination—a consuming desire—fueled by the anticipation and excitement of a future reward. It is a mind-set that can be created, fed, and increased in intensity from whatever state or condition one may be in.

In his book *Live Your Dreams*, Les states, "Wanting something is not enough. You must hunger for it. Your motivation must be absolutely compelling. Hunger will give you the courage to take your dreams and run with them."[1]

From my notes of our times together, here are some of Les Brown's hunger-increasing strategies.

HUNGER-INCREASING STRATEGIES

1. TAKE RESPONSIBILITY FOR YOUR LIFE: Stop blaming other people and past negative circumstances for where you are and what you have. It is up to you to accomplish your dreams.

2. GET AROUND SUCCESSFUL PEOPLE: Absorb their attitudes and spirits. Find out what motivates them. Observe how they are different from non-achievers.

3. READ AND LISTEN: Listen to motivational CDs or tapes and read inspirational material, such as the biographies of great people. Learn how others overcame great odds and what they did to achieve their goals.

4. OVERCOME YOUR LIMITATIONS: Don't let your fears hold you back. Unmask them and master them. Push them aside.

> **Power Point**
>
> "You must have a powerful reason to fight back in life."
> —Les Brown

5. VISUALIZE: Feed your subconscious. Regularly view pictures of your desired objectives.

6. DEVELOP A SENSE OF URGENCY: Take actions now that will move you toward your goals. Operate on a massive, relentless scale in order to accomplish your goals.

Les believes that "with a powerful hunger for your dreams driving you, you will be surprised at the ideas that will come, the people you will be able to attract, and the opportunities that will unfold."[2]

Power Point Question

Could you be doing more to increase your hunger for success?

"Blessed are they who hunger, for they will be fed."
—Matthew 5:6 (author's paraphrase)

Cadillac crashes into bedroom

A driver lost control of his vehicle, knocked over a stop sign, skidded across a lawn, and smashed into the bedroom of a woman who was asleep.

The desire for a Cadillac in her garage—not her bedroom—changed one woman's life. It caused her to begin a frantic search for uniqueness and knowledge in order to gain her dream.

It happened in 1955. *The $64,000 Question,* a popular quiz show, was the hottest program on television. On Tuesday nights, people watched the efforts of contestants attempting to win the top prize, which was a fortune at that time.[1]

As this woman watched the show, she believed that she was smart enough to be a contestant. She did not even dream of winning the $64,000 top prize. Her goal was to win the prize given at a lower level—a new Cadillac.

However, being selected to be on the show was a challenge. All the contestants were similar in only one respect: an incongruity in their lives. For instance, there was a shoemaker who knew all about opera and a burly marine who was a gourmet cook.

She analyzed her own situation. She was short, blonde, and pretty. She was also a psychologist and the mother of an almost three-year-old. There was nothing paradoxical about her, nothing that would catch the attention of the producers who chose the show's contestants. Then she realized that she could create her uniqueness. After much consideration, she decided upon the strategy of becoming an expert on boxing. That would be sufficiently opposite of her image to attract attention.[2]

The Power of Knowledge

The woman stated, "I went to work to turn myself into a boxing expert. I ate, drank, and slept boxing, its history, its statistics, its personalities. When I felt like I was ready, I applied to be on the show and was accepted. I went on and won. I came back and won again. I kept on winning until...I won the Cadillac."[3]

That wasn't all. She continued winning until she also won $64,000!

That event changed her life. Soon she was on television and radio programs and was making personal appearances. She was in show business and a whole new career took off.[4]

Who was this woman? **Dr. Joyce Brothers.**

> **Power Point**
>
> "I went to work to turn myself into a[n]...expert."
> —Dr. Joyce Brothers

Possessing knowledge might not win you a luxury car or cause you to be a quiz show champion, but it can release blessings and increase in your life.

Alvin Toffler said, "Knowledge...serves as a wealth and force multiplier."[5] This is true even in the sales arena. **Harvey Mackay** says, "The most powerful weapon anyone can possess in any negotiation is superior information and knowledge."[6]

Determine today to become more knowledgeable in the areas of your life where you desire increase.

Power Point Question

How much time are you actively spending on increasing your knowledge?

"[God says,] *My people are destroyed for lack of knowledge.*"
—Hosea 4:6

Governor Schwarzeneggar announces recovery plan

California's governor unveiled his recovery plan and called on the legislature to pass reforms so the state no longer spends more money than it receives.

Schwarzenegger knows that the state's spending will not be equal to its income unless the legislature makes balancing the budget a goal. The setting of goals causes one to focus time and energy on desired results. As admirable as this process might be, the setting of goals does not guarantee accomplishment. It only gives a government, business, or person a target.

For example, at the beginning of January, many people take time to list their goals and objectives for the coming year. With a rush of enthusiasm and fresh motivation, they excitedly dream and plan the accomplishments they anticipate in their finances and careers.

However, for many people, within weeks, this enthusiasm has diminished or has been lost altogether. A recent survey conducted in Britain said that "half of all people who make New Year resolutions break them within a month."[1] This happens because many of these plans, goals, and projects become bogged down in the "muddy marsh" of inertia. Others sink altogether in the "quicksand" of discouragement.

This result does not need to be your fate. You can greatly boost the probability of carrying out your resolutions by following these simple strategies:

STRATEGIES FOR ACHIEVING YOUR GOALS

1. BE REALISTIC: Set levels of achievement that are believable and attainable. If you succeed in achieving or going beyond these levels, that's great. Then you can set new goals.

2. Don't Set Too Many: If you try to change and/or improve too many things at once, you could easily become discouraged. It is better to identify one or two deeply seeded desires or needs for change and concentrate on those.

3. Set Goals in Multiple Areas: Don't get caught in the trap of setting only financial and career goals. Plan for increase in other areas: physical, mental, spiritual, important relationships, and giving.

4. Divide into Smaller Strategies: Avoid being overwhelmed by large tasks. Break down your big goals into smaller units. For instance, if your goal is to lose fifty pounds in the next year, go after four pounds per month or one pound per week as your action strategy.

> **Power Point**
>
> "The hardest rock will yield to those who drill with determination."
> —Jewish Folk Saying[2]

5. Keep Yourself Motivated: Do what is necessary to keep the desire for change strong. Display pictures representing your targets. Think about the benefits of succeeding. Keep positive input strong.

6. Avoid Excuses: Don't let misses become excuses for quitting. If you slip, then begin again.

7. Pray: Prayer is an empowering force that can help you to break old habits.

Keep in mind that even though the creation of goals is important, it is only through sustained action that you will experience change.

Power Point Question

How can you better sustain action for reaching your goals this year?

——————

"I press toward the mark."
—Philippians 3:14

Blind man robs bank, then cannot find way out

A man handed a threatening note to a bank teller and collected the money. He was quickly apprehended when the teller realized the man was blind. He asked her to help him leave the building.

After getting what he demanded, the robber asked the bank employee to help him leave the building. He failed in his misdeed because he did not plan ahead by considering a fundamental strategy to success: In almost everything, make sure you have an exit strategy.

I first became aware of the necessity of using such a strategy when I was a nineteen-year-old college student. During the summer break, I needed a good-paying job. I settled on driving a large delivery truck for a soda company in Los Angeles.

One day, I had to make a delivery to the back of a store. The only way to get there was to drive down a narrow alley. In order to enter the alley, I had to negotiate a wide turn in the street utilizing an empty parking space.

After making the delivery, I began to back up to leave. To my horror, I saw that a car was now parked in the "empty" parking space. I was hopelessly stuck in the alley until the driver returned and moved the vehicle. It was then that I became aware of the powerful principle of having an exit strategy. This principle has helped to guide my decisions throughout my life.

HAVE AN EXIT STRATEGY!

I employ this way of thinking in many areas of my life—from learning the location of the nearest emergency exit upon checking into a hotel room to leaving maneuvering room between my vehicle and the next car when I parallel park.

I use this strategy in the business arena. Normally, before entering into a transaction, I ask myself, *What will be our costs and/or options if this deal doesn't work? What is the exit strategy?*

There are times when exit-strategy thinking is not necessary and may even be counterproductive. However, there are other times when it is absolutely essential. Thinking this way does not imply a sense of untrustworthiness or a lack of commitment. It merely indicates that both parties are considering all possible outcomes before beginning a binding agreement.

Consider your own need for better exit-strategy thinking. Using this mind-set could help you to avoid needless heartaches, personal calamities, lost friendships, and vexing legal problems.

> **Power Point**
>
> "Before a wise man ventures into a pit, he lowers a ladder."
> —Samuel ha-Nagid, *Ben Mishle*[1]

Power Point Question

How can you better make exit-strategy thinking a part of your daily life and negotiating strategy?

"He will...provide a way out."
—1 Corinthians 10:13 (NIV)

Power Point #24

Stocks ignoring bad economic news

The market is better at accepting bad economic and corporate news, and investors are now focusing on the next earnings period in a positive manner.

Truly successful people are those who think positively and believe for good things. Even in the midst of gloomy news or the negative reports of others around them, they have trained themselves to maintain an undoubting attitude.

A DECISION ABOUT NEGATIVE REPORTS

A perfect example of such a person is **Bill Swad**. Bill is one of America's most successful automobile dealers. However, there was a time when he was not doing well financially. His life changed when he made a decision not to accept a negative report.

When Bill decided to get out of his economic rut, he was a baggage handler at the Columbus airport. He determined to accomplish his goal by going into the used-car business. At one of my Florida Increase Events, he shared the story of his opening-day experience.

"I borrowed money from a loan company to purchase three cars, and then I rented a small lot on a busy street. After hanging some light bulbs on a wire, I was ready for business. My sales shack was like a little greenhouse made out of wood and glass. However, I felt ten feet tall on the inside because I had made a total decision regarding my future, and I believed that I could do it.

"That first morning, the postman stopped by with some junk mail. He said, 'Mister, you probably ought to know that several businesses have started on this corner. Every one of them failed.'

"I wasn't about to let his negative beliefs ruin my future. I looked at the mailman and boldly exclaimed, 'Well, mister, this business is going to succeed.'"

Within three years, Bill was the biggest retail used-car dealer in the state. Next came new car dealerships. He became so successful that, at one time, he simultaneously operated the largest Chevrolet, Chrysler, and Nissan dealerships in the state of Ohio. In addition, he ran a large automobile leasing company and a finance company. Then he added an insurance company and two mortgage companies.

Bill succeeded because he was willing to take the risks, had a plan of action, and was determined to overcome obstacles. However, more than anything else, he succeeded because he would not let someone's negative opinion rob him of his positive attitude and expectations.

> ### Power Point
>
> "I wasn't about to let his negative beliefs ruin my future."
> —Bill Swad

"An attitude is the direction in which you lean," says **Lou Tice**, a noted author and teacher of superachievers. "An attitude is negative, if you anticipate negative outcomes, such as pain, displeasure, embarrassment, ridicule, failure, or hurt. An attitude is positive, if you look for and seek to possess the good that you perceive in situations."[1] He also says, "It takes time and repeated affirmations to change an attitude. However, once you change it, boom, you have let yourself go."[2]

Power Point Question

Are you letting negative attitudes keep you from pursuing your dreams?

"Choose life, that both you and your descendants may live."
—Deuteronomy 30:19 (NKJV)

Joe Gibbs rejoins Redskins

The NFL's Washington Redskins reached into their past with a most stunning move: They brought back the Hall of Fame coach who led the Redskins to three Super Bowl championships.

Joe Gibbs knows how to make good things happen. The first time he coached the Washington Redskins, the team made the playoffs eight out of twelve seasons. Also, his NASCAR racing teams have been among the most successful, winning two championships in the last four seasons.

Gibbs believes that the ability to create positive motion is one of the keys to effective leadership. Especially when a circumstance is negative or lethargic, one should seize it as "an opportunity to lap the field."[1]

Achievers need to have the ability, when the situation demands, to take control, activate the proper actions, break through the barriers of resistance, and embrace opportunities.

MAKING THINGS HAPPEN

I heard a good example of this action-oriented attitude at one of our seminars. It was shared by **Jim Money**, former head of the national employment company Snelling and Snelling Personnel. The story was about **Robert Townsend**, who was senior vice president of American Express before becoming the highly successful chairman of Avis Rent a Car.

A controller once told Townsend that he thought he could make American Express an extra $800,000 a day. However, he needed a special computer to calculate whether his plan could actually work. Townsend told the controller, "Get one now."

The controller replied, "If I turn in a requisition for one, it will take days, maybe weeks."

"I'll get you one," Townsend answered. He contacted the supply warehouse and found that they had one in stock. However, when he went to obtain it, the supply manager would not release it to him without a formal requisition.

"I've got something better than a requisition," Townsend declared. "Sign this."

"What is it?" the supply manager asked.

"It's my letter of resignation," explained Townsend. "I want you to sign this so that I can deliver it to the president of the company. When I tell him that I am resigning because a senior vice president of American Express can't get a computer from a supplier, he will know who you are."

He got his computer, and the controller used it to make American Express that extra $800,000 a day.

Sometimes, all it takes to cause a breakthrough is someone who will take the initiative and make things happen.

> Power Point
>
> "Seize [negatives] as an opportunity to lap the field."
> —Coach Joe Gibbs

Power Point Question

Have you empowered yourself and your key people to make the decisions necessary to seize opportunities?

"Prepare your minds for action."
—1 Peter 1:13 (NIV)

92-year-old woman gets 30-year mortgage

A bank in Australia has given a 92-year-old woman a 30-year mortgage to buy her first home. The woman became the country's oldest first home buyer.

This story is a great example of someone who is looking ahead to the future and activating her dreams. I find this forward-thinking mindset in the lives of almost all overcomers and great achievers. My friend **John Mason** shared on the subject of looking ahead at one of my Hawaii Increase Events. John is the best-selling author of several books and a gifted teacher.

"Probably the most common strongholds in a person's life are past mistakes and failures. Throughout history, great people, at some point in their lives, have failed. Only those who do not try anything, or expect anything, never fail. People who have few failures also have few victories."

DON'T LOSE TOMORROW'S OPPORTUNITIES

John also said, "We must learn to profit from past mistakes, be forward-focused, and invest in the future.

"Whatever stronghold the past may have on us, it can be broken. God does not hold us back. It is our own choosing that keeps us from moving forward. The more we look backward, the less able we are to see forward.

"In Philippians 3:13–14, the apostle Paul wrote, *'This one thing I do, forgetting those things which are behind, and reaching forth unto those things which are before, I press toward the mark for the prize of the high calling.'"*

DON'T LOSE TOMORROW'S OPPORTUNITIES

In his book *An Enemy Called Average*, John states, "Here is the key to being free from the stranglehold of past failures, hurts, and mistakes: Learn the lesson but forget the details. Don't roll over and over in your mind the minute details."[1]

John also says, "The past is history. It has no life—unless you continually breathe life into it. Today is the day to begin to shake off those shackles of the past and move forward to your future."

Power Point Question

Is some past negative event or memory keeping you from positive opportunities?

"Forgetting those things which are behind, and reaching forth unto those things which are before."
—Philippians 3:13

Man hit by lightning on golf course

A golfer who was struck by lightning was saved by a fellow golfer. His friend performed CPR until paramedics arrived.

After the golfer was revived, he said of his friend, "He gave me the gift of life." You also can give the gift of "life" to others—maybe not through CPR, but by speaking positive words into their dreams and self-images.

A teacher released this force into the life of **Rich DeVos**. DeVos is the cofounder of the world's largest multilevel marketing corporation and is also the owner of the Orlando Magic professional basketball team. At a convention where we were both speaking, he shared about how this power was imparted to him.

ONE OF THE GREATEST GIFTS TO GIVE

DeVos said, "One of the greatest things you can give to another person is the gift of encouragement. It is a gift with starting power and staying power. When I was struggling to find my way as a high school senior, my Bible teacher sent me to a life of significance just by writing a few words in my yearbook: 'With talents for leadership for God's kingdom.' Those words encouraged me to believe that God had a plan for me and my gift.

"That note was written to me more than fifty years ago, but it remains fresh even to this day. With those words echoing in my ears, I became determined to make a difference in life."

When I was at dinner with **Colin Powell**, America's former secretary of state, he shared how he endeavored to be an encourager: "I always show more kindness than appears to be necessary. Most people need this more than you will ever know."[1]

Zig Ziglar concurs, saying, "If you can catch people doing something well, no matter how small it may seem, and positively reinforce them for doing it, they will continue to grow in a positive direction."[2]

Richard Branson, who is the founder and president of Virgin Atlantic Airlines and Virgin Records, makes being an encourager one of his management strategies: "I praise, praise, praise. It brings out the best in people."[3]

> Power Point
>
> "Encouragement is a gift with starting power and staying power."
> —Rich DeVos

Being an encourager not only helps others, but it can also bless you. According to the late **Norman Vincent Peale**, "When you encourage others, you fill your own heart with courage."[4]

Be an encourager and give others the "gift of life."

> **Power Point Question**

How often do you publicly encourage people?

_____

"Encourage one another daily."
—Hebrews 3:13 (NIV)

Man comes out of coma

A man who had been shot in the head came out of his coma after seven years.

When my son, **Rock Harrison**, was seven years old, he came out of a coma—only it was a "learning coma." At least, that is what it seemed like.

Rock was intelligent and did well in most subjects. However, he had great difficulty with reading. He just was not proficient at connecting words in order to make phrases. Because of his deficiency, he was required to repeat the first grade.

His reading difficulties continued in second grade. In early spring of that year, I was informed by school officials that Rock's reading was still at preschool level. As a result, they planned to make him repeat second grade.

I was distressed. Rock was already the biggest and oldest boy in his class. I felt that holding him back another year could create a self-image problem that could negatively affect him for the rest of his life.

STRATEGIES TO CHANGE A SELF-IMAGE

While praying one night, I felt impressed to develop an action plan consisting of strategies to change my son's self-image and overcome his learning deficiency.

1. PRAISE: I began to praise Rock for the subjects in which he was doing well. I also reminded him of his past and current accomplishments.

2. LOVE: I reaffirmed to him that my love for him and acceptance of him was not based upon his performance, but rather on his relationship with me.

3. TIME: I rearranged my schedule so that I could give him extra time for reading assistance. I also set aside additional time for playing together and for personal attention.

4. AFFIRMATION: Since beliefs can be changed by repetition, I had him confess the truth of 1 John 4:4 several times a day: *"Greater is he that is in* [me], *than he that is in the world."* In addition, I would continually have him proclaim, "I am a winner!"

ASTONISHING IMPROVEMENT

Soon, I began to see improvement in his ability to read. He got better and better. Still, I was not ready for the great news that would soon come. At a follow-up appointment, school officials proclaimed that they had never seen such rapid improvement as they had with Rock. "In less than ninety days, he has skyrocketed from a preschool reading level to a mid-year third-grade reading level."

Rock advanced to the third grade. Plus, on the last day of school, he won the award for being the number one reader in his class!

> **Power Point**
>
> "Once a person's self-image improves, you will see significant gains in achievement."
> —Denis Waitley[1]

Power Point Question

What steps can you take to improve your own or someone else's self-image?

"Encourage one another and build each other up."
—1 Thessalonians 5:11 (NIV)

Toilet paper theft causes firing

Police used marked rolls of toilet paper to catch a principal who was stealing from his school. The markings, which could be seen only under ultraviolet light, proved the official was routinely taking school supplies home.

The principal in the above story had to resign in disgrace. While succeeding in developing his academic credentials, he apparently failed to develop his personal character.

Let's define character. *Merriam-Webster's 11th Collegiate Dictionary* defines character as "the complex of mental and ethical traits marking and often individualizing a person, group, or nation." Another definition of character I like is from former congressman **J. C. Watts**: "Character is doing what is right when no one is looking."[1] My personal definition of character is "the core thinking and values that predetermine a person's behavior."

Character is learned behavior. Good character is best taught at home by precept and example when children are young, as illustrated by the life of my friend **Jess Gibson**.

A TEST OF CHARACTER

Jess Gibson is an incredible motivational speaker and pastor from Springfield, Missouri. At one of my Increase Events, he shared about a test of character he faced when he was a teenager.

"At the age of fifteen, I had a before-school job at a local pharmacy. One morning, I was sweeping behind the counter where the cash register was located. All of a sudden, I saw it—a beautiful, crisp $10 bill. It was just lying there on the floor, waiting for me to pick it up. The boss was in the basement. No one else was in the store. Who would know? Should I or shouldn't I take the money?

"I thought about what I could do with ten dollars. Visions of candy and sugar plums danced through my head! Then it dawned on me. At that moment, my trustworthiness, my character, was being tested. How I responded to this temptation would shed light on who I really was and who I would become.

"I picked up the money, ran to the basement, and presented it proudly to the owner. He grumbled that someone had been clumsy handling money. He didn't even say thanks or give me something as a reward.

"However, I received my reward. It was that experience. It revealed to me that I was developing the positive character traits that would help guide me throughout my life and enable me to overcome bigger challenges and temptations."

Each action you take when faced with moral questions or temptations will help form your habits. These habits, in turn, will determine your character.

Power Point Question

How would those close to you describe your character?

"A good name is rather to be chosen than great riches."
—Proverbs 22:1

Car falls seven floors

A woman's car lurched through a thin steel barrier, became airborne, and tumbled from the seventh floor of a downtown Pittsburgh parking garage. Miraculously, the woman suffered only minor injuries.

If you have ever felt as if you were plummeting toward personal or financial destruction or that everything in your life seemed upside down, then **Dr. Robert Schuller** believes that his philosophy of living can help you.

A POSITIVE APPROACH TO LIVING

Dr. Schuller is the author of more than thirty books—five of which have made the *New York Times* best-sellers list. He is also the well-known pastor of the Crystal Cathedral in Garden Grove, California, from which he ministers worldwide every week by television.

On several occasions, I have had the opportunity to visit with him, and I have always been impressed with his energy, compassion, and wisdom.

As a young man, while pastoring a small church in Illinois, he somehow got on Dr. Norman Vincent Peale's mailing list. For three years, he received Peale's teachings on positive thinking. He says, "I became internally changed by all of the dozens and dozens of sentences in his sermons. I became a positive thinker."[1]

Dr. Schuller was convinced that he had a powerful message to give, particularly for people who were struggling with adversity in life. In 1955, "with his wife, Arvella, as the organist and $500 in assets, he rented the Orange Drive-in theatre and conducted...services from the roof of the snack bar."[2]

He began to help people by sharing his faith and positive approach to living with those who had never experienced life in that way. The church continued to grow until now it has one of the largest congregations in America—plus millions watching weekly on television.

Dr. Schuller says that he became a possibility thinker one day when he was reading his Bible and some words of Jesus leaped off the pages at him: *"Nothing will be impossible for you"* (Matthew 17:20 NIV). Therefore, all things are possible.

To Dr. Schuller, possibility thinking is simply "focusing faith on achieving definite goals."[3] This thinking is evidenced in his Possibility Thinker's Creed:

> **Power Point**
>
> "When faced with a mountain, I WILL NOT QUIT!"
> —Robert Schuller

THE POSSIBILITY THINKER'S CREED

When faced with a mountain,
I WILL NOT QUIT!
I will keep on striving
until
I climb over,
find a pass through,
tunnel underneath,
or
simply stay
and
turn the mountain
into a gold mine
with
God's help![4]

Dr. Schuller believes that really "nobody has a money problem. They only have an idea—a thinking—problem. Get the right thinking and ideas—the money will be attracted to you."[5]

> **Power Point Question**

What are you doing to activate possibility-thinking power in your life?

"Nothing will be impossible for you."
—Matthew 17:20 (NIV)

Families left out in the cold

Most people are absorbing the rising cost of energy. Some are having to choose between buying food and paying to heat their homes.

A s a young man, **James Harris** did not have to make the kind of decision that the above families are needing to. He was homeless.

James grew up on the South Side of Chicago in a neighborhood where poverty was a way of life and hopelessness was all around him. He was the middle child of nine siblings. His mother was an alcoholic, and he never knew his father. He had no male guidance around him, so he sought direction from the wrong people. His role models were pimps, drug dealers, and gamblers.

At the age of twelve, James began to drink alcohol and smoke marijuana. Over time, the cycle of getting and using drugs caused him to become a walking zombie. His family did not trust him, his friends were long gone, and he had nowhere to live. He ate out of garbage cans. Abandoned buildings became his haven of survival. He would crawl into the corners of these buildings and fend off any rats or other animals that felt he was intruding in their space.

One evening, he almost froze to death. As a result, he placed himself in a drug rehabilitation program in nearby Zion, Illinois.

James also became active in a local church. After a season of service and training, he was ordained as a deacon. At church, he met a lovely and charming lady, Alicia, who became his wife.

While we were driving together to a service one day, James told me that, at about that point, he experienced another milestone in his life when he was given my teaching series entitled *Awakening the Great Multitude Mind.* He said, "What you taught was revolutionary and life-changing, to say the least."

As a result of the teaching, the image that he had in his mind of who he was and what he could accomplish was changed. He determined to transform his life and his future. He studied and obtained a realtor's license and soon thereafter earned a life insurance agent's license.

James excitedly told me, "In my first four years of marriage, I was able to purchase investment properties that caused our net worth to be close to a million dollars. We now live in a beautiful home, and both of us drive BMWs. In comparison, to this day, none of the other eight siblings in my family owns a home or a car."

> ## Power Point
>
> "Increase thinking can cause benefits beyond measure."
> —James Harris

This story vividly illustrates a success power point shared by **Rabbi Daniel Lapin**: "In order to acquire more money, you need to work on... changing yourself. It may not be easy, but it can certainly be done, and it works."[1]

Power Point Question

How can "increase thinking" cause you to experience a more fulfilling life?

"As a person thinks in his heart, so is he."
—Proverbs 23:7 (author's paraphrase)

Government feeds and cares for monkeys

To prevent the spread of infectious diseases, monkeys that are imported into America are quarantined for observation for a month. While in captivity, these monkeys must be fed and cared for.

Y ou are helping too much if you take responsibility for the care and feeding of other people's monkeys," says **Dr. Kenneth Blanchard**, coauthor of the *One-Minute Manager*.

In this context, the term "monkey" refers to the tasks, jobs, or problems that are the responsibility of other people, such as subordinates, friends, or children.

When you give in to the temptation to take on problems or jobs that are not yours, in essence, you "put a monkey on your back." This happens when you find yourself saying, "Let me help," or worse yet, "Let me do that for you." The other person may walk away feeling thirty pounds lighter because you just took away his or her monkey. However, you now feel weighed down because the "monkey" is yours to care for.

Blanchard teaches that the two biggest reasons to avoid taking other people's monkeys are: (1) they must be cared for and fed by you; (2) their former owners now check to see how *you* are doing with *their* monkeys!

If you put too many of other people's monkeys on your back, it will add stress to your life and reduce the time available for your main responsibilities.

Keeping the Monkeys Off Your Back

In my *Time Increase* CD series, I teach three responses that I learned from Blanchard for keeping other people's monkeys off your back.

1. BE UNDERSTANDING: Tell the person that you understand the complexity of the problem and that you feel for him or her. Say that you are willing to talk about how the individual (not you) can get it solved.

2. OFFER SUGGESTIONS: Inform the person that this is his or her responsibility, but also give some suggestions, strategies, and/or ideas to try.

3. GIVE STRATEGIES: If you feel that the other person does not have the ability to handle the monkey, give specific directions. Explain the next move or strategy that you would recommend, and then supervise what the person does.[1]

> **Power Point**
>
> "Monkeys belong with their rightful owners, not an adoptive parent."
> —Dr. Kenneth Blanchard[2]

By learning how to keep monkeys off your back, you can prevent your life from becoming a zoo!

> **Power Point Question**

What strategies can you use to keep other people's monkeys off your back?

"And Moses' father-in-law said to him, 'The thing that you are doing is not good. You will surely wear out.'"
—Exodus 18:17–18 (NASB)

Man watches TV for five years

A man sat in front of his television set for five years. His landlord eventually discovered him with a television listings magazine still on his lap. The Christmas tree lights were still working, but the TV had broken down— and he was dead.

I have heard that the practice of watching TV can be a time-waster, but *five years?* Of course, this man had died. However, many people who are very much alive watch too much TV and/or indulge in activities that have no apparent redemptive value.

An achiever should attempt to eliminate or at least reduce those actions and activities that, in reference to pursuing their dreams and goals, are non-productive.

Dr. Robert Rutherford teaches that "a person cannot effectively deal with wasted or nonproductive time until he understands the concept of 'mortgaged time.'" Dr. Rutherford is a popular seminar teacher who specializes in the areas of negotiation and time management. His teaching on mortgaged time has been of great benefit to me.

UNDERSTANDING MORTGAGED TIME

At one of my Increase Events, Dr. Rutherford stated, "There is never enough time to do all the worthwhile and valuable things in life. There is nothing that you can do to get more time. You have exactly 168 hours a week. Since time is precious and irreplaceable, choices must be made. If you promise or commit some of these hours to a person, institution, or task, these hours are now not available for other uses. You have 'mortgaged' your time.

"Your time gets mortgaged because of the commitments you make. These time agreements you make may be visible and may have been done consciously, or they may be more subtle, invisible, and not easily recognized by you. However, whether they are created by conscious decision or by actions and/or habit patterns, they are still real.

> **Power Point**
>
> "Time is precious and...choices must be made."
> —Dr. Robert Rutherford

"Understanding that you have options as to what you do with your time is the beginning of effective time management. Taking responsibility for these agreements—and considering them in advance of commitments—will enhance your productivity and the quality of your life."

Here are some strategies from Dr. Rutherford that can help you deal with mortgaged time:

1. AWARENESS: Continually be aware of the agreements you are creating that will impact your time and scheduling.

2. COMMUNICATE: Let others know how you feel about these agreements, and what you believe they are—and are not.

3. DON'T GET STUCK: Sometimes, agreements that worked for you in the past might no longer be supportive of your dreams and goals.

4. RENEGOTIATE: If you are committed to agreements that are no longer productive or meaningful, honor your agreements. At the same time, try to renegotiate or eliminate the ones that are not working.

By activating the above strategies, you can increase productivity while experiencing a more enjoyable and fulfilling life.

Power Point Question

What time/mortgage agreements should you alter or eliminate?

"[Make] *the most of your time.*"
—Ephesians 5:16 (NASB)

Quarterback leaves Pro Bowl early

The NFL's starting quarterback left the game—and the stadium—early in order to catch a plane from Hawaii to home.

E ven though his playing time had ended, this quarterback stirred up a ruckus when he left for the airport while the game was still in progress. However, he smoothed things over by saying, "I apologize for leaving early, but I just could not wait to get back home to my family and fans."

By describing the reason for his departure in such a masterful manner, this player showed his command of a sales and debate strategy referred to as "reframing." I define *reframing* as "changing the frame of reference that someone is using to perceive or interpret an experience." The underlying concept is that if you can change people's interpretation or perception, you can change their response and corresponding feelings.

UNDERSTANDING THE REFRAMING TECHNIQUE

Overcoming resistance and gaining understanding using the strategy of reframing can work in both the marketplace and in the personal arena, as evidenced by an experience I had with my oldest daughter, Sandy.

Several years ago, Sandy, who was a teenager at the time, was working in our front yard. Two young men drove up and talked to her from their car. After several minutes, she came up to the house and asked if she could go out with them that night.

Replying that I had never met the boys and knew nothing about them, I suggested that she invite them to our family dinner the following week so all of us could get to know them better.

My response greatly upset Sandy. Her face turned red, and she blurted out, "What's wrong, Dad? Don't you trust me?"

Knowing that she was feeling very negative about my answer, I immediately put my reframing mind-set to work. I explained, "Honey, if I had a million dollars in a briefcase, and some stranger came to the house and wanted to borrow it for the evening, would I let him?"

She replied, "Of course not. You would protect it."

"Then you can better understand my response. It is not that I don't trust you. I'm trying to protect you. To me, you—and your reputation—are more valuable than a million dollars in a briefcase."

Immediately, her countenance changed. She became teary eyed as she hugged me, saying, "Thank you, Dad, for loving and caring for me so much."

> **Power Point**
>
> "The person who sets the frame of reference will be the one with the most influence."
> —Anthony Robbins[1]

By effectively using the strategy of reframing, I had quickly changed a situation from negative to positive.

If you can change how people think about an event or an occurrence, you can automatically change how they feel about it. This is why you should have the strategy of reframing in your verbal arsenal.

Power Point Question

How can you better use the strategy of reframing?

"You are looking at things as they are outwardly."
—2 Corinthians 10:7 (NASB)

With low-cal movement, less is more

A recent study found that people can significantly reduce their odds of dying of heart disease and extend their longevity by cutting calorie consumption.

Increase—and survival—often go to the sleek and efficient, not the bloated and ponderous. Believing this truth is one of the things that made **Robert Crandall** so successful. Crandall was chairman of American Airlines from 1982–1998. Under his leadership, American broke out of the pack to become one of the world's largest airlines.

FLYING PLANES THAT ARE TOO BIG

During the time that Crandall was running the airline, he sat across the aisle from me on a flight to Tulsa. We had a wonderful talk about the things I liked and didn't like about American's AAdvantage Frequent Flyer Program and the service of the carrier as a whole.

A few months later, I noticed one of his success strategies at work. At a press conference, he announced that American was disposing of most of its fleet of jumbo jets and replacing them with smaller jets—Super 80s and 737s. When asked why he was doing this, he replied, "No airline has ever gone broke by flying planes that are too small. Airlines go broke by flying planes that are too big."

With this statement, he released a powerful point to consider. Increase thinkers are prepared to grow and expand as needs demand. However, increase thinking does not always mean that bigger is better. In the case of this airline, it meant something quite different.

American's consumer surveys had revealed to the management that —except on long haul flights—its flyers were more interested in increased frequency of jet departures than in plane size. By flying smaller jets, the airline could offer more flights and at different times. Also, the airline realized that it was much easier to fill smaller jets, resulting in higher load factors and correspondingly greater profits.

I have lost count of the number of times that I have consulted with and prayed for various business leaders and pastors who were in financial difficulty. Analyses of these situations revealed that it was solely because they built facilities that were too big and expensive or because their overhead was too large.

Jesus taught about this concept. In John 15, he shared how a grapevine's long-term output was actually increased through pruning (cutting back) the branches. Because of this cutting back, the branches could receive more nourishment and strength from the roots. This, in turn, caused more and bigger fruit to be produced.

While you are increasing, be careful not to get too big. Also, be ready to temporarily cut back in certain areas if it will result in greater future growth.

As best-selling author **Laurie Beth Jones** says, "Dinosaurs became extinct; rabbits still abound."[1]

Power Point Question

Are there areas—such as overhead, facilities, staff, debt, or inventory—in which you should reduce costs now in order to increase profits later?

"Every branch that does bear fruit he prunes [trims] so that it will be even more fruitful."
—John 15:2 (NIV)

Palm Desert buys university

The California State University system opened its newest campus in the Palm Springs area.

There was something very unusual about the opening of this institution of higher learning. This university campus opened without the state putting up any money for land or buildings.

For several years, local officials tried to get the state university system to open a campus in the Coachella Valley area of Southern California, where Palm Desert is located. At the time, residents had to drive over fifty miles if they desired to attend classes at a university site. Repeatedly, they were told, "If the state has to pay for it, it will take decades. In fact, it might never happen."

Two local residents would not accept that answer. They teamed up to do something highly unusual. They arranged for the chancellor of the California State University system to come to town for a luncheon with some dignitaries. They also invited several local residents and professional businesspeople. When the chancellor informed them that a new campus was not planned anytime soon, someone asked, "What if we donated a campus to you—lock, stock, and barrel? Then would you open it and furnish the staff?" At first, the chancellor thought it was a joke. No one had ever donated a whole campus before. When he realized that they were serious, he answered, "Yes."

That began the process. They met with city officials, and they agreed to donate a 200-acre site of land for the campus. Then, by combining municipal money with private donations, in ninety days, the two raised $9 million for the first building. While it was being constructed, another $10 million was raised, and a second building was completed. Then, the third building was finished.

Now, over 1,000 students are attending classes. Oh, and the two private citizens are still raising money to keep the construction going.

INTENTION + MECHANISM = RESULTS

These two individuals are using a success formula that I first learned from my friend **Brian Klemmer**. Brian is a master of group dynamics and a seminar facilitator. At one of my Hawaii Increase Events, he taught about a formula that achievers use to make things happen. The formula is Intention + Mechanism = Results.

Brian maintains that the key to making things happen is for one to change focus. Instead of concentrating solely on the "how to" (mechanism), put your focus and energies on the hunger/desire (intention). When someone's intention to do something is strong enough, the various mechanisms will begin to be manifested.

Brian teaches that "one way to raise the intensity of your intention is visualization. To achieve your goal of creating something new, you must surround yourself with pictures of the desired finished state. That will cause your subconscious to work on creating mechanisms to raise money to achieve your goal."

Using the above formula can help you to unlock the powerful potential of your subconscious and accomplish what may seem impossible or insurmountable.

Power Point Question

What can you do visually to increase your intention?

"Write the vision, and make it plain."
—Habakkuk 2:2

Bugging devices cause political furor

Listening devices were found in the offices of the mayor of Philadelphia. The FBI acknowledged that it was responsible for planting the bugs.

A political furor erupted following the disclosure that a Democrat, who was in a bitter election battle with a Republican, had his offices bugged by a department of the federal government that is headed by a Republican. The FBI stated that the bugs were placed as part of a criminal investigation and were not political espionage.

If the thought of federal officials "bugging" the offices of an elected official alarms you, consider this story: Some time ago, one foreign country's security intelligence agency warned its top businesspeople not to fly a certain European air carrier. The reason: They discovered that the airline's first- and business-class sections had bugs—electronic bugs. Not only that, but it was also reported that undercover agents were posing as flight attendants in order to steal corporate secrets from the unsuspecting business travelers who were on their planes.[1]

In another case of possible bugging, "a recent court case revealed that the FBI used the popular OnStar [information and emergency assistance] system [that comes on many new cars] to...monitor private conversations."[2] Unknown to most people, within the OnStar system is a passive listening feature, which gives it "the ability [potential] to eavesdrop on unsuspecting motorists."[3]

Also consider the fact that many of the new cell phones on the market come with internal cameras. This technology enables someone to discreetly and quickly record anything from unpublished financial data to a CEO's faux pas at the company holiday party. Those images can be transmitted via e-mail to a competitor or media outlet in a matter of seconds.[4]

Or even closer to home, the last time you signed on to the Internet, it is possible that someone could have recorded what you wrote or bought and then shared that information with various marketers, other curious parties, or even the news media.

SAFEGUARDING CONFIDENTIAL INFORMATION

The point of all these stories is this: The more successful you become, the more vulnerable you are to bugging. Therefore, it is imperative that you give greater importance to protecting the confidentiality of your conversations and documents.

If you do not implement safeguards, then private information may become available to competitors, dishonest or superambitious employees, or anyone who might steal your briefcase, snatch your laptop computer, or visit your office after hours.

Conduct a security vulnerability inspection. Develop systems and policies that will minimize your risk of unintended information distribution, corporate piracy, or identity theft.

A "bug problem" could cause more than a political furor; it could cost you your reputation and/or business.

Power Point Question

Do you or your company have a security awareness problem?

"Discretion will protect you, and understanding will guard you."
—Proverbs 2:11 (NIV)

Parents made kids eat rats and roaches

Chicago police arrested the parents of four children who had been abused and fed boiled rats and deep-fried roaches.

The average person is appalled to read about such abuse by parents. Yet I wonder how many parents feed their children verbal rats and roaches.

Many psychologists believe that if children (or spouses or employees) are continuously yelled at and told that they are dumb, clumsy, unattractive, or can't do anything right, negative self-images will be formed in their minds.

SELF-IMAGE REPRODUCES ITSELF

Robert Schuller said, "The need for dignity, self-worth, self-respect, and self-esteem are the deepest of all human needs. Unsatisfied, it will result in boredom, restlessness, and is the dawn to dangerous adventures. Unsatisfied, it will drive one to destructive actions and dishonest manipulations. A person's self-image will always reproduce itself in action."[1]

Zig Ziglar affirmed this belief, stating, "A person cannot perform as a winner if he does not see himself as a winner."[2]

Some time ago, I heard a story from Greek mythology that illustrates this point. Pygmalion was a king who sculpted a beautiful statue of a lady out of ivory. He then fell in love with it. Aphrodite, the goddess of love, shot an arrow into the statue's heart, and it came to life.

From this story comes what is referred to as the Pygmalion Theory. This theory states, "People will become like the image that is conveyed to them."

Probably more than anything else, the words of others form and shape an individual's self-image. Just as one's diet of food can make one physically well or sick, the diet of words that one receives can make one mentally or emotionally well or sick.

Therefore, each of us needs to be aware that the opinions we give and the words that we speak to others will either add to or take away from their self-images. Again, this is a key reason why **Colin Powell** makes it a practice to speak positive words to people. He told me, as I wrote earlier, "I always try to show more kindness to people than appears to be necessary. Most people need this more than you will ever know."[3]

> **Power Point**
>
> "People will become like the image that is conveyed to them."
>
> —Pygmalion Theory

JAWS OF LIFE

Fire departments in many cities possess a mechanical device called the Jaws of Life. This tool can cut through doors or twisted wreckage in order to free trapped victims. Your mouth is like that tool. It can be a powerful force of hope and encouragement, freeing victims trapped by negative circumstances and poor self-images. Determine today that you are going to be a person who has the "jaws of life."

Power Point Question

Do you consistently build up others?

"A word fitly spoken is like apples of gold in settings of silver."
—Proverbs 25:11 (NKJV)

New lease on life

A man who went to jail at the age of seventeen becomes the first in his family to earn a college degree.

When Andre—the man in the above story—decided with his friends to rob someone at an ATM, it seemed like a good idea. Yet all he got was $43, a few credit cards, and a prison term. A football coach gave him a second chance, however, and now he has a dream for a new future. He is graduating from college and plans on becoming a coach, saying, "That man gave me a new lease on life."

Sometimes, all someone needs is a fresh opportunity. This is true not only for those who have made wrong decisions, but also for those who have had a loss.

My mother, who recently passed away at the age of ninety-one, was such a person. She experienced the sudden and untimely death of my father when she was sixty. When Dad died, it was as if her joy and purpose for living left also. She said, "In losing my husband, I felt like Job of old: I had lost everything."

A NEW LEASE ON LIFE

Mom worked her way out of her season of despair. She decided to help others who had lost loved ones through death, separation, or divorce. She began conducting monthly meetings at her home for hurting people. They would gather together for a time of sharing and prayer. Her gatherings were called "New Lease on Life."

Because of the success of these meetings, her home gatherings expanded to other cities. Eventually, they became an organization with chapters across America.

In her book, *A Second Chance at Love,* Mom shared the inspiration that led her out of her despair: "In contrast to the philosophy of God helping those who help themselves, I found that oftentimes He helps those who can't help themselves. God meets us at our point of weakness.

"Trying to recover in our own strength leads to weariness and failure. As long as I focused on the 'I' rather than the 'I Am,' I was disillusioned....It took a complete surrender to God for me to find peace with myself.

"That was my turning point. Once I allowed Him to begin the resurrection in my life, God began to work in ways that were beyond my wildest dreams. He showed me that helping others would also help me. It is a strange but proven biblical principle, 'Give and you shall receive.'"

> **Power Point**
>
> "God meets us at our point of weakness."
> —Edna Harrison-Harlin

Mom did receive satisfaction and joy from helping others. She also received something else. A retired rear admiral, who was a widower, came to one of the meetings. They started dating and shortly thereafter became happy newlyweds. Soon, they were traveling together across the globe.

My mother's life changed for the better when she put her focus on others. So will yours.

Power Point Question

List three things that you can do this month to help those who are hurting.

"Satisfy the needs of the oppressed, then your light will rise in the darkness."
—Isaiah 58:10 (NIV)

Man hugs tree to escape fine

A New York City deli owner was given a $1,000 fine because he chained his bicycle to a tree in front of his store.

Commissioners stated that the man was guilty of "tree abuse." However, they agreed to forgive the fine if the owner consented not to abuse the tree again. In addition, the man was required to hug the tree for news photographers.

Hugs might not greatly affect trees, but there is growing evidence that people respond favorably to touch and hugs.

My friend **Dewey Freidel**, who is a seminar speaker and motivational coach for pro athlete teams, actually teaches on the benefits of hugging.

Dewey states, "Something as simple as a hug or touch can make a big difference in someone's life. Many people spend time stroking their cats or dogs. Meanwhile, their spouses and children are across the room literally starving for their affection or a touch."[1]

A meaningful touch is a "gentle pat, a stroke, or a hug given to or received from a significant person."

HOW IMPORTANT IS A HUG OR TOUCH?

In a study conducted by Purdue University, the researchers asked librarians, as students were handed their library cards, to "accidentally" touch every other student. Afterward, the students were interviewed. All the students who had been touched as they were handed their cards gave researchers favorable comments about the library and the librarian.[2]

In another study, Dr. Dolores Krieger, a professor of nursing at New York University, conducted research proving that there is a physiological benefit to touching one another. The study showed that when a person receives a positive touch, that person's hemoglobin levels instantly rise. Hemoglobin is the pigment in red blood cells that carries oxygen to the body. As a result of touch, oxygen is released in greater proportions into the blood stream, causing energy to be immediately released. Touch was also shown to help people recover from sickness quicker.[3]

Hugging has been even shown to improve marriages. Laurence Roy Stains and Stephan Bechtal did a national survey of 2,102 women for their book *What Women Want*. In the study, the women reported that when their husbands took time to hug and kiss them, other than when they were in the bedroom expecting sex, they felt that they were respected and adored for their own sake.[4]

However, there is one caution. According to best-selling author **Mark Victor Hansen**, "In our culture physical contact between two people who barely know each other might be considered taboo. However, done correctly, a hug is a perfect way of immediately giving and receiving love from another human being."[5]

Use wisdom, but make meaningful touches and proper hugging a part of your daily routine.

> **Power Point**
>
> "[Receiving] a hug...can make a big difference in someone's life."
> —Dewey Freidel

Power Point Question

How many positive touches and hugs are you giving out a day?

"People were bringing little children to Jesus to have him touch them."
—Mark 10:13 (NIV)

Amateur golfer shoots 59

The golfer described his feelings as "surreal" and "in disbelief" after he shot a record-breaking 59 on a par-72 golf course at a resort in California.

The man in the above story inspires people to achieve greater success in golf. My friend **Peter Lowe** inspires people to achieve greater success in life.

Peter's Get Motivated seminars attract audiences of 20,000, 30,000, and more. He has been featured in *Time, USA Today, Selling,* and *People* magazines and on CNN.

In 1981, Peter heard me speak at a meeting in Vancouver, Canada. At the time, he was selling microcomputers and calculators to businesses. Although he enjoyed sales, he was not fulfilled. He thought, *"If I became the greatest salesman in Canada, it would not make me happy."*

Peter wanted his life to have an impact on the lives of others. He made the decision to become a sales trainer and motivator of people.

When he conducted his first seminar, he had an audience of four people (including his mother). During his early years of speaking, Peter had to memorize his presentations word for word. But he was diligent, faithful, and committed. Even in the face of unbelievable obstacles and intense competition, his meetings got bigger and bigger. In just ten years, he went from starting his business to becoming the most popular conductor of success seminars in the world, drawing the largest audiences.

From my notes of our times together, here are some of his success strategies.

PETER LOWE'S SUCCESS STRATEGIES

1. PERSEVERE: "A person cannot become really successful in anything until he or she determines not to quit."

2. BE DILIGENT: "Watch the details. I personally analyze at least thirty pages of computer reports every day in order to maximize attendance and income."

3. SUSTAIN PROPER INPUT: "Keep yourself on a consistent and regular feeding program of books, tapes, and seminars. Fellowship with other achievers."

> **Power Point**
>
> "Most achievers do not feed themselves enough."
> —Peter Lowe

4. THINK PIGGYBACK: "We increased our revenues greatly by offering program options, such as a VIP seating section and idea-exchanging lunches."

5. BE AWARE OF TIMING: "There is a right time to change things. Often, the timing of something is as important as what is done."

6. BE CONSISTENT: "You may change your tactics and methods, but stay with your core principles and calling."

7. LEARN FROM OTHERS: "A wise person learns from his mistakes. A wiser person learns from the mistakes of others."

8. PLAN LONG TERM: "Success takes time. I am much more interested in where I will be in five years than I am in the next seminar."

I got insight into another one of Peter's success strategies when I asked him, "How did you come to be the one who is putting on the largest success seminars in the world?" He replied, "I put on the best small seminars in the world."

Power Point Question

What are you doing to rise to a higher level of success?

"Wise men lay up knowledge."
—Proverbs 10:14

Dead woman sheds a tear

Doctors were stunned when a woman they thought was dead shed a tear.

Upon seeing the woman's tear, the emergency-room team brought the woman, whose vital signs had ceased, back to life. Afterward, she stated, "God has given me a second chance."

I had an experience in which my wife "came back to life." However, it was not a resurrection of physical life but rather a restoring of life to our marriage.

For thirty-seven years, I was privileged to be married to an incredible woman. She was the most positive, happy, caring, vivacious person I have ever known. Until her untimely death in May of 2000, she filled my life with joy and love.

Cindy Harrison was my childhood sweetheart. We married young, and to others we appeared to have a perfect relationship. However, behind the scenes, we were dealing with some serious relationship problems. It all came to a head shortly before our tenth anniversary. Cindy ran into the bedroom, fell down on the floor, and, with tears streaming down her face, screamed out, "God, what do I do? I don't love him anymore."

Cindy later commented, "Our crisis was not caused by any one big thing. Bob was always faithful, and he provided well for the family. Yet, at that time in his life, he had a negative attitude. He was always criticizing me and others. Plus, he had gotten so busy with business and sports that the kids and I were not getting the attention we needed.

"Because of these things, I began to get negative about him. Without either of us fully realizing what was happening, my negative attitude caused love to fly out of our home like a bird flying out of its nest."

That day, while Cindy was on her knees, a Bible verse came to her remembrance. It was Philippians 4:8: *"Whatsoever things are of good report;...if there be any praise, think on these things."*

CINDY'S GOOD-REPORT LIST

Cindy continued, "Pulling out a piece of paper, I began to activate the two words *'good report.'* I wrote down the things I liked about Bob—the things he was doing right.

"Every morning and every night, I read, confessed, and added to that list. I began to see more good things about him and our marriage. My thinking and attitude began to change. Soon, my feelings and emotions responded. Fresh love sprang forth, and our marriage became better than ever before.

> **Power Point**
>
> "One comes to believe whatever one repeats to oneself."
> —Robert Collier[1]

"Bob and I would never have had a second chance at love except for my tearful decision to resurrect dead love by choosing to become a person of good report."

Power Point Question

How many things can you itemize on a "good-report list" of your spouse, parents, or key business associates?

"Whatsoever things are of good report..., think on these things."
—Philippians 4:8

Last Oldsmobile rolls off line

Ending a 107-year history for the brand, the final Olds automobile rolled off the assembly line in Lansing, Michigan.

What is the best way to handle change when it involves the end of something? While at dinner one night with retired **General Norman Schwarzkopf**, I learned a great strategy regarding this aspect of life.

The commander of American troops for the Desert Storm war with Iraq joined some friends and me in St. Louis. I asked him, since he had retired and was an in-demand motivational speaker, if he missed being in the military. He replied, "I miss the camaraderie with the troops and the rich relationships that I had in the military, but I am greatly enjoying my new life."

Then the general stated, "One of my secrets of success in life is this: I believe that most situations in life are temporary and that...life is a collection of seasons."

A COLLECTION OF SEASONS

What a simple but powerful approach to life. Our lives revolve around seasons. The changing of seasons determines when a farmer plants, waters, and takes in the harvest. It also dictates what kinds of clothes a mother purchases for her children and whether a vacationer heads to the mountain slopes for snow skiing or a mountain lake for waterskiing.

Likewise, during the course of our lives, a change of careers, relationships, competitive products, or even physical capabilities can require a change of actions, obligations, and responses. Life is really a series of beginnings and endings that often require different goals, activities, resources, and relationships.

General Schwarzkopf went on to say, "Losers and victims try to hang on to a season after it is over. Winners and achievers cherish the memories and experiences of the old season but embrace the new season that is ahead."

This concept of life being a collection of seasons greatly helped me when my wife, Cindy, unexpectedly passed away in her prime. We had enjoyed a wonderful life together. However, I had to acknowledge that the season of sharing our lives together was over. Although I would miss her, I needed to embrace my new season of being single. I realized that the sooner I adjusted to this reality, the better dad I would be to my children, and the more capable I would be in impacting the lives of others.

> **Power Point**
>
> "Life is a collection of seasons."
> —General Norman Schwarzkopf, USA, Retired

The writer **Henry David Thoreau** gave this advice: "Live in each season as it passes; breathe the air, drink the water, taste the fruit, and [enjoy] the influences of each."[1]

Learn to recognize when seasons change, and make adjustments accordingly. You will reduce stress, release fresh increase, and have a jump start on the future when you flow with the changing seasons of life.

Power Point Question

What can you do to bring "seasonal thinking" into your life?

—————————

"To every thing there is a season."
—Ecclesiastes 3:1

Governor says "thanks" to firms

The governor of a Midwestern state returned from a two-day trip to the Northeast. He traveled there to personally thank the executives of four major companies for their ecnomic investments in the state.

A chievers must be very careful that they do not get so busy and focused on achieving that they forget to be grateful and thankful. Because of demanding schedules and the hustle of daily routines, it is easy to overlook the thoughtful, productive, and caring acts of others.

How important is it to praise the performances of subordinates? Consider the words of **Charles Schwab**, who was paid $1 million (back when a million dollars was really worth a million) to run the nation's largest steel empire: "I consider my ability to arouse enthusiasm among people the greatest asset that I possess. The way to develop the best that is in people is by showing appreciation and encouragement."[1]

Zig Ziglar agrees: If you will give everyone the recognition and rewards they deserve, he says, "then [you] have taken a giant stride in becoming Top Performers."[2]

Bill Marriott, the president of Marriott Hotels, also believes in the power of encouragement. He says, "The two most important words in human relations are thank you."[3]

Make gratitude a part of your motivational arsenal. A personal note is such a tool. **Rich DeVoss**, cofounder of Amway Corporation, believes "people can accomplish great things when they are encouraged by positive and hope-filled messages."[4]

It takes only about three minutes to write a note, fold it, and stick it in an envelope, but the power of that note can be awesome. Personal notes build relationships, which are the most important element in any business.

Also, people who send thank-you notes are thought of as gracious and well-mannered. Additionally, since so few people send them, doing so puts you as a clear cut above the rest.[5]

Here are some keys for better showing appreciation.

HOW TO BETTER SHOW APPRECIATION

1. SAY THANKS NOW: Form the habit of verbalizing appreciation the moment it is appropriate.

2. ACKNOWLEDGE THE CONTRIBUTIONS OF OTHERS: Give unexpected recognition—gifts, flowers, or notes of appreciation—even when it is not a special occasion.

3. CELEBRATE THE SUCCESS OF OTHERS: On special occasions, do something a little extra for people. When someone experiences something out of the ordinary emotionally, it creates an "emotional implantation" on the brain. This experience becomes an interpreter of future thoughts and actions. By spending a little extra time and money celebrating other's special moments, you can bless them. In addition, you create positive imaging of yourself, your company, and/or your product.

> **Power Point**
>
> "The two most important words in human relations are thank you."
> —Bill Marriott

Make being grateful one of your success strategies. Be more concerned with how you treat people than how you impress them. You and others will be happier and have more productive days.

Power Point Question

How can you better show appreciation for your family and staff members who have helped you in some way?

"Be ye thankful."
—Colossians 3:15

Charity gets moving in new van

A rental company is providing a local charity with a van. The donation will enable the nonprofit organization to continue to offer their services to the needy for at least another year.

Anthony Robbins and some of his friends were in New York City. They needed a van—not for a year but for an afternoon. They desired to deliver meals and gifts to needy families on Thanksgiving Day. The only problem was it was a holiday weekend and all the rental places were either out of vans or closed. Then Anthony got an idea.

I was visiting one of his seminars in Chicago when he shared this inspirational story about perseverance. Anthony turned to his friends and boldly said, "Look, the bottom line is this: If we want something bad enough, we can make it happen! All we have to do is begin to take action. The problem is not that there are no vans in New York City. The only problem is that we don't have one."

Fresh with that awareness, the group determined to get a van. First, they tried walking out in front of vans that were driving down the street. Although they waved their hands, the drivers not only didn't stop, they swerved around them and sped up.

Then they tried waiting by a traffic light. When a van would stop for a red light, one of them would walk over and say, "Today is Thanksgiving. We'd like to help some needy families. Would you drive us to a certain underprivileged area here in New York City?" No one they asked was willing to do that.

Then they tried offering the different drivers $100 to transport them. That got people's attention. However, when the drivers were told the area where the members wanted to go, they all said no.

PERSEVERING THROUGH NEGATIVE RESPONSES

Robbins' friends were about ready to give up when he exclaimed, "It's the law of averages: Sooner or later, somebody is going to say yes."

Shortly thereafter, another van drove up to the traffic light where the group was standing. It was extra big and could accommodate all of them. When they asked the driver to help them, he said, "I'd be happy to take you." He reached over, grabbed a cap, and put it on his head. They were all astonished when they noticed what was written on it: "Salvation Army."

The man drove them to a grocery store, and then they all went out and spent the afternoon blessing people.

This story is a good illustration of not giving up in the face of negative responses. As Anthony Robbins says, "Successful people...kept asking, kept trying,...because they knew that sooner or later they would find someone who could satisfy their needs."[1]

> **Power Point**
>
> "Successful people...kept asking, kept trying."
> —Anthony Robbins

Sales Trainer **Tom Hopkins** also teaches this concept in his seminars: "A person is not judged by the number of times that they fail but by the times they succeed. Success then is in direct proportion to the number of times that one fails but keeps on trying."[2]

Power Point Question

What shortages or obstacles have been preventing you from a desired outcome?

_____

"Why stand ye gazing?"
—Acts 1:11

Cruise ship runs aground

A sternwheeler passenger ship developed steering problems while cruising about 80 miles upriver from Portland, Oregon, and ran aground.

Gavin and Patti MacLeod's ship also ran aground. Their personal "love boat" crashed on the rocks of divorce.

Gavin, who is a celebrated actor, has played leading roles on television series. He is probably best known for his role as the captain of *The Love Boat*. He met Patti while taking tap-dancing lessons in a class she was teaching. Gavin says, "I loved Patti from the time we first met."[1]

After they were married, Gavin's demanding schedule and weeks away from home took their toll. One day, he sent her a letter and asked for a divorce.

Patti says, "The experience of divorce was worse than anything I had ever been through. It was worse than my father leaving the family when I was a little girl, worse than my mother's death. She felt pain twenty-four hours a day."[2]

Finding herself hurt and in confusion, she started seeing therapists. They advised her to forget Gavin and get on with her life. On the other hand, some of her close friends kept telling her that, if she still loved Gavin, she should "hang on" and that "God is a God of restoration."

Choosing to believe that God would heal their broken relationship, she began to earnestly pray for herself, her husband, and their marriage.

Not long afterward, Gavin unexpectedly called and asked her to attend a social event. She suggested that, instead of going out, maybe he would like to come over to her home for dinner.

When Gavin arrived and stood in the doorway, Patti greeted him with her now-classic line, "Your dinner is a little cold. It's been waiting three years."

The couple began dating again. Soon thereafter, they were remarried. Every time that I am with them, either socially or at a television studio, they radiate joy, happiness, love, and energy. Now, by sharing their experience in meetings and on television, they bring hope, joy, and laughter to others around the world.

From our times together, here are some of Patti and Gavin's marriage success strategies.

PATTI AND GAVIN'S MARRIAGE SUCCESS STRATEGIES

1. CELEBRATE TOGETHERNESS: Embrace activities as a team. Go places together, meet friends together, make decisions together.

2. GIVE EACH OTHER SPACE: Don't try to possess or control all the other person's time or activities. Set aside time for each of you to do the activities you individually enjoy.

> Power Point
>
> "Friends don't hurt each other but talk things out."
> —Gavin and Patti MacLeod

3. BE CARING: Friends do not deliberately hurt each other. They talk things out. Demonstrate by your words and actions that your partner's wants and needs are important.

4. PRAY TOGETHER: Everything that happens in a day can be influenced by those precious moments spent together in the presence of God.

According to Patti, by making these strategies the foundation of their relationship, they are more in love than ever before.

Power Point Question

How many of the above strategies are you actively using in your marriage?

"[The husband] must love his wife as he loves himself, and the wife must respect her husband."
—Ephesians 5:33 (NIV)

City starts automated trash removal

Honolulu's new refuse service features trucks equipped with mechanical arms. The driver collects and dumps trash from standard-sized, city-supplied 96-gallon trash bins. This process makes it quicker and easier to collect trash.

The city of Honolulu has developed a process that makes it quicker and easier to get rid of trash. Paper pile-up can be a big problem, not only with cities, but also with individuals.

Being surrounded by piles of paper can cause stress that smothers creativity and brings feelings of anxiety and loss of control. An achiever can use up so much energy dealing with an influx of mail, memos, and periodicals that he or she loses valuable time—time that could be better spent nurturing and training people and/or doing other important tasks.

Success guru **Peter Drucker** teaches, "All work takes place in time and uses up time. Yet most people take time for granted. Nothing else, perhaps, distinguishes effective executives as much as their tender loving care of time."[1]

Professional organizers say that the key to increasing productivity by eliminating paper messes is to develop a personalized system—one that works and makes sense for the individual. The main concept behind any paper reduction system is based upon giving priorities to incoming paper flow.

Motivational speaker **Patrick Morley** teaches that priorities "are pre-decisions that we make in advance that decide what we give our time and attention to. Priorities become the grid that helps us to distinguish opportunity from distraction."[2]

My friend **Al Andrews**, who is the former chief financial officer of Lockheed Aircraft, believes that "without a well-thought-out plan to direct you specifically, you will get off course."[3]

The key strategy behind any effective program is this: Avoid stacking incoming papers in a pile to be dealt with later. Everything needs to have a place, wherever that may be.

Here are some effective strategies for paper reduction.

STRATEGIES FOR PAPER REDUCTION

1. ACT ON IT: Create a "hot folder" for urgent matters. If something is important and you must personally take care of it, get it done as quickly as possible.

2. REFER IT TO SOMEONE: If it is important but can be handled by someone else, forward it to that person.

3. SAVE IT/FILE IT: Some items must be referred to in the future. Develop an easy-to-use retrieval system to help locate documents quickly when needed.

4. THROW IT AWAY–REDUCE IT: Some of what you receive is not applicable or important. Open your mail standing next to a trash container. Better yet, have subordinates sift through the mail and forward only important items and articles to you.

> **Power Point**
>
> "Small efforts can add up to giant results."
> —Anthony Robbins

5. HALT IT: The less you receive, the less you have to deal with. Cancel subscriptions that are not beneficial.

Activating these strategies can free you for new levels of creativity and productivity while increasing your desktop space. As Anthony Robbins teaches, "Small efforts can add up to giant results."[4]

Power Point Question

What systems can you create for better paper-flow management and elimination?

"Let all things be done decently and in order."
—1 Corinthians 14:40

Graham awarded Congressional Medal

Billy Graham was awarded the Congressional Gold Medal, the highest honor Congress can give to a civilian.

Billy Graham has been called "the nation's premier revivalist." Graham has filled sports stadiums around the world with the simple message that people need spiritual fulfillment in their lives. For over fifty years, this influential figure's words have reached television audiences, churchgoers, and U.S. presidents. He has been featured more than thirty times on the Gallup Poll's annual "World's Most Admired Men" list.

For a number of years, Graham has had Parkinson's disease. This condition has made it impossible for him to drive a car or write by hand, but he is making the most of his days. He is still conducting crusades and appearing on television. An estimated 2.5 billion people around the world tuned in to watch the Billy Graham television special, "Starting Over."

I was privileged to be at the special banquet honoring Graham with the Congressional Medal. The ceremony was attended by members of the house and senate, as well as **Bill Clinton**, who was then president of the United States. The award was given for "outstanding and lasting contributions to morality, racial equality, family, philanthropy, and religion."[1]

At the banquet, President Clinton stated, "Billy Graham has touched hundreds of millions of lives. He has helped many people in positions of power and influence keep, or regain, their bearings. To me, he is a model of Christian charity."

Former president **George H. W. Bush** shared that Graham was also a great help to him: "I cannot tell you what Billy Graham's presence, and his faith, meant to me as president and commander-in-chief. His beliefs and faith gave me great strength."[2]

SUCCESS SECRET: A GOOD CHARACTER AND REPUTATION

One of Graham's secrets of success is his reputation for integrity and right living. His commitment to living a life of character has given his ministry longevity.

For example, in 1948, while conducting meetings in California, he and his staff created and agreed to abide by what they called the "Modesto Manifesto." Graham described the agreement as a "shared commitment" to integrity and purity in which they would, among other things, avoid "financial abuses" and "any situation that would have even the appearance of compromise or suspicion."[3] From that time, Graham did not "travel, meet, or eat alone with a woman other than [his] wife."[4]

> **Power Point**
>
> "When character is lost, all is lost."
> —Billy Graham[7]

My friend **Edwin Cole**, who authored over fifteen books before his death, stated, "Character is not the same as personality. Personality is seen in public; character is built by what you do in private. There are 'has beens' in every area of life—music, movies, television, sports, and ministry. Many of these people built their personalities, but neglected their character. When a person's personality wears off, only their character remains."[5]

Make having a good reputation a foundational part of your life. In the words of College Basketball Hall of Fame Coach **John Wooden**, "Ability and talent may get you to the top. It takes character to keep you there."[6]

Power Point Question

How can you increase the power of your reputation?

———

"Create in me a clean heart."
—Psalm 51:10

Asian elephant born in captivity

Riccardo has become the first second-generation Asian elephant ever to be born in captivity.

Riccardo was born at the Center for Elephant Conservation, a private 200-acre facility operated by the Ringling Bros. and Barnum and Bailey Circus. Since 1992, the circus' breeding program has had 16 elephant births, including Riccardo's parents. Because of the scarcity of Asian elephants, Ringling Bros. is breeding its own elephants, many of which will eventually perform in the circus. In this way, the circus is planning ahead to secure a key element of its future. Ringling Bros. recognizes that, in order to ensure continued success, they must make plans for the future.

My friend **Myles Munroe** believes that "there is no future without planning."[1] Myles is an international motivational speaker, best-selling author, lecturer, and consultant for governments and businesses. He teaches leaders how to maximize their potential.

He says, "Most people try to live their lives without any real thought of planning. They are like a contractor trying to construct a building without a blueprint. As a result, their lives are out of balance and unreliable... plus they end up unsatisfied and frustrated."[2]

Myles states, "I am a stickler for planning. Anyone who works for me will tell you that I have plans for next week, next year, and five years from now."[3]

One of the key strategies used by **Lee Iacocca**, former president of Chrysler Corporation, was planning ahead. At a time when Chrysler was in the midst of astronomical cash shortages, asset liquidation, massive layoffs, and possible bankruptcy, Iacocca set aside $750 million to launch a new product—the Caravan. A reporter asked him why he did it. Iacocca replied, "I had to. If you eat the seed corn, you have no future."[4]

Microsoft founder **Bill Gates** believes that this strategy is one of their company's keys to success. He states, "The key trade off is how much money to put into present consumption versus how much you put into future products and improvement."[5]

MAKE INVESTMENTS IN YOUR FUTURE

In the personal arena, as well, those who are wise plan and make investments in their future. Instead of spending all their income, they choose to set aside a certain amount for their future needs and retirement.

Planning and budgeting for the future does not come naturally in our "I want mine now" society. The key is this: Make delayed gratification a part of thinking and planning. Otherwise, you will find yourself fighting recurring battles with debt, relationship problems, health difficulties, and shortages.

If you desire to live a lifestyle of increase now and in the future, then determine to set aside—regardless of circumstances—a certain amount of your present time, energy, and money as "seed" for future harvests.

Power Point Question

Which activities and involvements would you change if you better focused on planning for the future?

"Consider [the ant's] *ways and be wise!...it stores its provisions in summer and gathers its food at harvest."*
—Proverbs 6:6, 8 (NIV)

Woman rides out tornado in bathtub

When a tornado ripped through her town, a local woman jumped into her bathtub seeking protection.

As the tornado shattered the woman's house, the fierce winds blew the tub into the woods. When the storm had subsided, the woman crawled out of the tub, suffering only some bruises and scratches during her ordeal.

One evening, my friend **Sue Boss** experienced a different kind of storm. Rather than destroying her home, it ripped through her heart and shattered her life.

A group of people from the church she attended was returning from seeing a passion play in Eureka Springs, Arkansas. Her son was on his motorcycle. Following him was her husband, who was riding with the church's pastor on his bike.

Apparently, her son, who had been up studying all the night before, fell asleep. His cycle crossed the centerline and hit an 18-wheeler truck head-on. The impact with the truck killed the boy instantly. The collision also damaged the front axle of the semi, causing the driver to lose control of his rig. The truck then crossed the centerline. It struck the second bike, killing her pastor and her husband.

Sue says, "I was just numb. Most of my family was gone—in one day. Not only did I have to suffer from this devastating loss, but I had to deal with other issues. I didn't know if we had $10 or $10,000 in the bank, or if we even had life insurance. Also, there was a good possibility the trucking company was going to sue me."

Through all that she faced, Sue's faith in God undergirded her in her season of grief. It gave her comfort and hope for the future.

Sue became very active in a local church, volunteering to help others in need. This giving of herself helped her to work through her grief. It also provided the venue where, sometime later, she met a sharp businessman who was a widower. After a season of courtship, they were married.

Today, the couple serves as pastors of a thriving church in Austin, Texas. The church has a strong community outreach and buses hundreds of kids to special monthly youth events.

When I was at dinner with **General Norman Schwarzkopf**, he made a powerful statement about handling negative events: "In life, there will be setbacks. The real key to success is the ability to get back up."

Former Dallas Cowboys coach **Tom Landry** shared the same viewpoint, stating, "Your reaction to adversity will determine your success or failure."[1]

What transpired in Sue Boss's life demonstrates a great truth. Even after it appears that dreams have been destroyed, one can experience a beautiful future.

> **Power Point**
>
> "The real key to success is the ability to get back up."
>
> —General Norman Schwarzkopf, USA, Retired

Power Point Question

Has a negative experience or loss been holding you back or causing you to think about giving up?

"Though I walk through the valley of the shadow of death, I will fear no evil: for thou art with me."
—Psalm 23:4

Family disappears on the road to nowhere

An Illinois family's disappearance on a New Mexico highway has stumped police. Authorities say their vehicle apparently turned off the main highway onto a side road and then vanished.

"If you want to have a successful enterprise [or trip], you must clearly know where you are going."[1] So says best-selling author **Stephen Covey**.

Not knowing where they are going is the problem of many people. They are riding the merry-go-round of life: They are moving and changing horses but are not going anywhere.

Earl Nightingale believes that this is one reason why goal setting is so important: "People with goals succeed because they know where they're going."[2]

Covey refers to this goal-oriented mind-set as "Success Habit #2: Begin with the End in Mind." It refers to the strategy of never beginning anything before determining the desired end result.[3] When someone adopts this type of thinking, he or she realizes the importance of making both the beginning and the ending of things memorable and significant.

MAXIMIZE THE BEGINNING AND ENDING

At the age of seventeen, well before Covey's book was written, I first became aware of the importance of this concept. I had won the competition to become drum major and lead my high school marching band in its football half-time shows. In addition, I was given the responsibility of creating each show's theme, plotting out where each band member would be positioned during each formation, and then teaching the band members the formations and maneuvers needed for successful presentations.

During the preceding summer, I had attended drum-major training school. The headmaster stated what he believed to be the number one strategy for a successful show: "Focus on the beginning and ending. Make sure those two elements are done well, and you'll do okay."

Power Point
"Start with a clear understanding of your destination." —Stephen Covey[4]

Throughout the football season, I concentrated on those formations. The band received rave reviews and wild enthusiasm over their performances.

Since that time, I have endeavored to make this beginning-and-ending thinking a mind-set of my life. I try to have a good beginning and ending in everything I do—whether it is delivering a speech, eating a meal, having a family outing, or even going about my daily routine. As a result, my life has more meaning and the things that I do have a greater impact, creating a lasting impression.

Implement end-in-mind thinking as a regular part of the planning and execution of your activities. Your life will take on a new dimension of power and direction.

Power Point Question

Before you begin something, have you clearly defined how to begin and where you want to end?

"I make known the end from the beginning."
—Isaiah 46:10 (NIV)

Cities finding gold in parking fees and fines

For many municipalities, revenues from parking fees and fines now rival property taxes as a major source of income.

These cities are not really finding gold in their parking meters. However, they are discovering a great source of extra income. Businesses across the globe are doing the same. They are discovering that they can create great sources of additional income by adding goods and/or services to their already existing product offerings.

As an example, after a trial study, Hilton Hotels installed mini-bars in all their rooms. The corporation found that guests who used their mini-bar units spent an average of $3.40/night. Soon the hotel chain was making more than $14 million in annual sales from its mini-bars with a profit margin of around 38 percent. That came to approximately 5.3 million extra dollars.[1]

This hotel chain was effectively using a powerful income-enhancing strategy that I refer to as "product-added increase."

PRODUCT-ADDED INCREASE

Product-added increase is based on the concept that by piggybacking new products or offerings with existing products or offerings, additional sales and profits can be created.

For instance, years ago, when I was operating my Chrysler dealership in Southern California, I used this strategy. Realizing that we needed to create sources of income in addition to our normal profits from car sales and service, I utilized piggybacking.

After some investigating, I found that there were some optional services we could make available to our customers at the time of sale. These would help the customer and also produce extra income for us. Soon we were offering extended warranties, life and accident insurance policies, and vehicle service contracts. The income from these extra offerings became significant. In fact, there were some months when the extra profits from these offerings made the difference between the dealership being in the black or the red.

I have noticed this product-added strategy being used by many airline reservation agents when they ask if they can also assist with car-rental reservations. That simple question produces thousands of dollars in extra income for the airlines every year.

My friend **Peter Lowe**—who is billed as "America's Premier Success Seminar Conductor"—used this strategy. He added a VIP seating section and celebrity lunches, thereby increasing his profits per seminar.

You, also, may be able to increase your profits by adding extra products and/or services to your lineup.

Power Point Question

How could the strategy of piggybacking increase your profits?

"I am the LORD thy God which teacheth thee to profit."
—Isaiah 48:17

Nails removed from man's head

A carpenter stumbled on scaffolding and fell onto a coworker who was using a nail gun. As the two fell to the ground, the man's nail gun began to fire, hitting the other carpenter six times in the head. Over several days of operations, doctors were able to remove all the nails.

In order to avoid a fatal infection, the nails in this man's head had to be removed. There is a different kind of "infection" that can set into churches, clubs, businesses, and families—and it may also be "fatal." It is the negative attitude of an employee or member.

This kind of infection normally begins when someone within the organization, group, or relationship becomes upset by some other member's actions or a perceived injustice. Instead of giving the situation time to change or correct itself, the disgruntled individual begins to manifest his or her negative feelings through criticism, disrespect, pouting, temper tantrums, or hostility.

If not handled quickly and properly, this negative attitude can spread to others in the group, business, or family. If left untreated, this "infection" can be harmful to harmony and unity.

Best-selling author **John Maxwell** teaches, "What starts as a bad attitude in one or two people can make a mess of the situation for everyone. Bad attitudes must be addressed. They will always cause dissension, resentment, combativeness, and division. And they will never go away on their own. They will simply fester and ruin the team."[1] He also says, "If you leave a bad apple in a barrel of good apples, you will always end up with a barrel of rotten apples."[2]

In dealing with these negative-attitude situations, consider the following strategies:

INFECTION PREVENTION KEYS

1. BE PROACTIVE: If you discover that someone is upset or negative, deal with the situation as quickly as possible.

2. GO TO THE SOURCE: Try to discover the root cause and attempt to deal with it rather than just reacting to the symptoms that are being manifested.

3. COUNTERACT THE NEGATIVE: Discuss the positive aspects of the situation or give a different point of view to the person.

4. CONTAIN THE OUTBREAK: Recognize negativism as a contagious infection that needs to be treated while it is still localized and has not spread to others.

> Power Point
>
> "If you want outstanding results, then you need good people with...awesome attitudes."
> —John Maxwell

5. PERFORM SURGERY: If the above avenues fail to correct the situation, make the changes needed to cut out the cause or carrier of the negativism.

Determine that you are not going to ignore negativism. Deal with it in a firm but compassionate manner before it infects others.

As John Maxwell states, "If you want outstanding results, then you need good people with great talents and awesome attitudes."[3]

Power Point Question

Do you have a negative-attitude situation that you need to deal with?

―――――――――

"Now I beseech you, brethren, mark them which cause divisions."
—Romans 16:17

Man gets free trip to Hawaii by jogging

A Phoenix man revealed that he makes money while jogging. As he runs, he picks up coins lying on the sidewalks and streets. Having found over $5,000 in loose change, he used some of the money to pay for a vacation in Hawaii for his wife and himself.

Many people believe that, to experience increase, they must discover, do, or win something big. In reality, great increase often comes as a result of faithfully doing things that might seem small or insignificant.

Such is the case with **Tim Storey**. Tim is an in-demand motivational speaker and the founder of the Hollywood Bible study, which regularly attracts over 500 celebrities and movie industry personnel for evenings of learning and inspiration. Tim spoke at one of my Increase Events, at which he made this statement: "You will find that the big things in life are normally found in the middle of the little things."

WHERE TO FIND THE BIG THINGS

Several years ago, Tim was working with The Power Team. The Team was a group of bodybuilders who performed onstage feats at school assemblies and convention centers across the nation. They combined their acts with motivational and/or spiritual messages. Tim was in charge of grocery shopping, pressing uniforms, stacking ice, buying water bottles, and so forth. He has stated that he was diligent, faithful, and always did the best he could.

One day, as he was walking through the lobby of a hotel, a nationally renowned minister spotted him and called him over to visit. The minister was so impressed with Tim's attitude and apparent good work ethic that he hired him. Soon Tim was traveling around the world as this man's personal assistant.

On one particular trip, the minister could not make it to one of his overseas meetings. He called Tim and informed him that he would have to be the speaker at the meeting. Tim found himself addressing a crowd of over 18,000 people. He says, "That day, I realized—I wasn't a water boy anymore."

> **Power Point**
>
> "Big things...are normally found in the middle of... little things."
> —Tim Storey

Now, Tim travels all over the world and is greatly impacting our generation. It all began because, while he was faithfully doing the little things, something big appeared.

Faithfulness is a learned behavior. It is a habit of achievers that begins when they honor their commitments, tend to details, and always do the best job possible in all that they set their hands to do.

For instance, I once asked my friend **Peter Lowe** how he came to put on the largest success seminars in the world. He responded, "I put on the best small seminars in the world."

By better activating this strategy, you may not only get a free trip to Hawaii, but you will also experience greater increase throughout your life.

Power Point Question

How good are you at handling details and taking care of the little things?

_____

"He that is faithful in that which is least is faithful also in much."
—Luke 16:10

Woman trapped in elevator for three days

A Hong Kong woman was trapped in a broken elevator for three days before she was discovered and freed. After 60 hours, she emerged hungry, thirsty, and tired.

My friend **Aaron Lewis** had a fearful incident involving people who were trapped.

Early one bitterly cold winter morning, he was driving home with his two youngest children. The kids had gone with him while he drove his wife, Tiwanna, to the downtown Hartford hospital where she worked.

He told me the story of what happened next. "The snow was six inches high, and I realized that I could not drive all the way into my driveway. The garage was only a few feet away, so I figured that I would leave the little ones in the car as I grabbed a shovel out of the garage in order to clear a path in the driveway. I left the engine running so that the kids would not get too cold.

"Within seconds, my two-year-old son, Israel, had unstrapped himself and locked the automatic door locks. "I pleaded with my son, 'Unlock that door now or I am going to give you a spanking.' He yelled back, 'No, no, no.'

"To make matters worse, he then reached over and turned the heat to the highest setting. I became afraid that this would make his little sister, Madonna, ill. Next, he cranked the radio volume up high. Then, he started the windshield wipers. After that, he activated the blinkers and the signal lights.

"Fearing that he might put the car in gear during his antics, I ran into the house to find the extra key. I could not find it anywhere.

"Racing back to the car, nightmarish possibilities of negative outcomes whirled through my head. I was now beginning to panic. If anything happened to those small children, it would be my fault. Government authorities might take the kids away from us due to neglect. I might end up in jail."

THE ANSWER IS WITHIN YOU

Aaron continued, "Then I stopped, took a deep breath, and said a simple prayer: 'Father, help me to find an answer.' Suddenly, I heard within me a voice saying, 'The answer is within you.'

"It was then that I became aware that the key I needed was not necessarily a physical key. Maybe it was a mental key—a strategy. Then the answer came to me.

"I calmly made a deal with my son, saying, 'If you open the door for daddy, he will give you a candy.' He reached over and unlocked the door."

> **Power Point**
>
> "The answer to most problems lies within us."
> —Aaron Lewis

Aaron believes that "throughout life, there will be challenging situations. We will conquer most of our battles if we realize that the answer to most problems lies within us."

Power Point Question

How can the principle in this story help you to better solve problems?

———————

"You teach me wisdom in the inmost place."
—Psalm 51:6 (NIV)

Dallas Cowboys coach was pure class

Tom Landry, who coached an NFL record 20 consecutive winning seasons and led the Dallas Cowboys to two Super Bowl championships, passed away at the age of 75.

Tom Landry was a living legend. More than any other person, he helped to establish the image of the Cowboys as "America's Team."

Years ago, I had the opportunity to speak with him at a success seminar in El Paso, Texas. We rode together in the limo to the airport and discussed what Tom had taught that day:

THREE KEYS TO CREATING A WINNING TEAM

1. KNOW YOUR OBJECTIVE: "You must have a clear-cut, well-defined objective. Very few people really know what they want."

2. HAVE AN ACTION PLAN: "Setting a goal is not the main thing. It is deciding how you will go about achieving it. This plan must be written and measurable."

3. IDENTIFY YOUR RESISTANCE: "There will always be forces of resistance released against your action plan. The purpose of these forces is to keep you from accomplishing your objective."

In teaching about resistant forces, Tom went beyond the success strategies that are normally taught, such as setting goals, staying motivated, and remaining positive. He believed that, because they fail to identify the forces of resistance that are working against them, many teams, as well as people and companies, are defeated. Once resistant forces, plans, or plays are identified, then strategies can be developed to overcome—or at least minimize—their effectiveness.

Tom thought in terms of defense. He became a defensive player and coach for the New York Giants when he was only twenty-nine years old. Since he was young, he could not establish his authority based on age or experience. Also, others had more athletic talent and football skill than he did, so those things could not be his foundation, either.

Tom became a specialist in understanding the defenses of other teams. He would spend countless hours learning about opposing players and teams. He devoured anything and everything he could find concerning football.

Tom stated, "A leader doesn't have to be the smartest member of a group, but he does need to demonstrate a mastery of his field. Mastery means more than just knowing data and facts; it requires an understanding of the information and the ability to apply that information to the situation at hand."

In the vehicle that day, Tom explained, "A successful leader must be one step ahead of the crowd. Knowledge of resistance forces, combined with proper preparation, enables one to be innovative and overcome opposition."

Power Point Question

Have you identified the resistance forces working against your action plan?

"Wise men lay up knowledge."
—Proverbs 10:14

Can found inside of fish

A Norwegian man had a surprise when he cut open the codfish that he had caught. Inside of the fish's stomach was a soda can.

Yan are on the road to greater success if, inside of you, are "cans." The cans that I am referring to are positive affirmations that come out of your inner being in response to challenges, problems, or negative situations.

"WE ARE WELL ABLE"

There is a great story in the Bible about how the lack of a can-do attitude dramatically affected a large group of people. The tribe of Israel had escaped from the bondage of Egypt and arrived on the banks of the Jordan River. Their leader, Moses, sent twelve spies to report on the conditions in the Promised Land.

Ten spies returned with negative reports about the land. These spies focused on the obstacles—walled cities, giants, and the fact that they were outnumbered—and all the reasons why they did not believe they could conquer and win. They exclaimed, *"We are not able"* (Numbers 13:31 NKJV).

The other two spies, Joshua and Caleb, saw the same challenges. However, they declared that the obstacles didn't matter because the God who had brought the people out of the bondage of Egypt and parted the Red Sea was with them. They announced, *"We are well able"* (Numbers 13:30).

The ten spies and the people chose to accept the reasons why they could not conquer and win. Therefore, they never entered into the land that God had provided for them. On the other hand, forty years later,

Joshua and Caleb led the people's children to the Promised Land, and they possessed it.

The main difference between Joshua and Caleb and the other spies was a can-do attitude.

Motivational speaker **Les Brown** concurs: "You must know within yourself that if others can overcome and live their dreams, then so can you."[1] Many times, it is not the problems that you face that make the big difference; it is your attitude toward them. Remember that—

INCREASE COMES IN CANS

If you think you are beaten, you are;
If you think you dare not, you don't.
If you like to win, but you think you can't,
It is almost certain you won't.

If you think you'll lose, you've lost,
For out of the world you'll find
Increase begins with a fellow's believing—
It's all in his state of mind.

If you think you are outclassed, you are;
You've got to think higher to rise.
You've got to believe in yourself before
You can ever win the prize.

Life's battles don't always go
To the stronger or faster man;
But sooner or later, the man who wins
Is the man WHO THINKS HE CAN!
—Unknown

Power Point Question

How could you get more "cans" to come out of your mouth?

"We are well able to overcome."
—Numbers 13:30

Postal truck plunges into pool

When a U.S. Postal Service driver apparently forgot to secure the brakes of his vehicle, the truck rolled down a hill, crashed through a fence, and plunged into a residential pool. It was estimated that at least 1,800 pieces of mail were in the water.

Checks belonging to you might not be going to the bottom of a pool, but they could be going to the bottom of someone's pockets. If there are areas in your personal and/or business life in which you are vulnerable to breaches of security, this could be happening to you. How costly this vulnerability can be is demonstrated by the following true story.

"We are short $90,000 in parts inventory!" is what a worried Toyota dealer told Bill in an urgent phone call. Bill, who was the president of a sales audit company, immediately scheduled an appointment at the dealership to review the records of its service department.

He found that more than a thousand tickets for automotive parts sales were missing. He then discovered that an employee who sold parts was throwing away numerous sales tickets for cash items each week and pocketing the money. The amazing thing was that the dealership had instituted a program to prevent this kind of theft. A dedicated and loyal employee in accounting had been assigned the task of keeping a Missing Parts Ticket Log.

Then how did this loss occur? Unbelievable as it may seem, the accounting employee had never been instructed in what to do when she discovered that there were missing tickets. She just faithfully noted the missing ticket numbers in the log.

Even more startling is what Bill discovered over the next sixty days. Fresh from the memory of this embezzlement, he audited more than a hundred other dealerships, specifically checking for missing parts sales tickets. To his surprise, he found the following:

ARE YOU INVITING THEFT?

1. One-sixth of the dealerships had no system to record ticket numbers at all.

2. One-third of the dealerships had the same person who received cash from customers keeping track of missing tickets.

3. And, most amazingly, not one—yes, not one—of the hundred dealerships audited had checked their Missing Ticket Log Report in the previous three months.

Every one of these businesses was inviting theft and embezzlement because it either did not have, or did not maintain, a proper inspection system.

You may think that you could never have this kind of problem, but consider the fact that even Jesus did. John 12:6 states that Judas, one of Jesus's twelve disciples, served as treasurer, and that *"he was a thief; as keeper of the money bag, he used to help himself to what was put into it"* (NIV). If Jesus was susceptible to embezzlement, then so are you.

As I teach in my *Time Increase* CD series, "People do what is inspected, not what is expected."

> **Power Point**
>
> "People do what is inspected, not what is expected."
> —Bob Harrison

> **Power Point Question**

What systems do you have in place to protect the key areas of income, expenses, cash flow, customer data, and inventory?

"Riches can disappear fast...so watch your business interests closely."
—Proverbs 27:23–24 (TLB)

Student jailed for udder nonsense

School officials charged a seventeen-year-old honors student with disruption of a school function because he wore a cow costume to classes on the last day of school. The senior was led away from his high school in handcuffs by police.

My friend **Eastman Curtis** needed more than a cow costume to attract attention at a school. Curtis, who is a motivational speaker and speaks at high school and college assemblies across the nation, needed a strategy in order to turn around a negative situation.

Eastman was scheduled to speak to a college assembly right after the students' lunch break. He had brought two young men with him who were former world champion tag-team kickboxers. As they walked into the assembly center, they were startled to find that there were only three people in the auditorium. At one of my Increase Events in Florida, Eastman shared how he dramatically changed the situation.

"I was not willing to accept the empty auditorium. Knowing that students had to be around somewhere, I called my two kickboxer friends over and said, 'Come on. I've got a plan.' Rushing over to the school cafeteria, we found it cram-packed with humanity.

"I jumped up onto a chair and yelled, 'Hey! Attention! Can I have your attention, please? For today, and today only, we have with us two former world-champion kickboxers! They are about to put on a kickboxing exhibition you won't want to miss, right now in the auditorium. Follow me.'

"Several of the students started screaming, 'Yeahhh!' As we left the cafeteria, I felt like the Pied Piper! I looked behind me and saw that there were at least a hundred students following us.

KEEP THINGS IN MOTION

"These two friends of mine, who hadn't practiced kickboxing in years, went on stage and just started beating the mess out of each other. Knowing that a fight will draw a crowd every time, I left the doors open, cranked up the PA system to its maximum, and started yelling, 'FIGHT! FIGHT! THERE'S A FIGHT IN HERE!' More people started running to the auditorium from everywhere. Soon the place was packed. Then, when my friends were done, I quickly got up and shared my message."

> **Power Point**
>
> "A body in motion tends to stay in motion."
> —Isaac Newton

Eastman activated a powerful success strategy that is based upon a law of physics given by Isaac Newton: "A body in motion tends to stay in motion." **Anthony Robbins** believes that this strategy is a key ingredient of achievers: "Successful people...kept asking, kept trying."[1]

If you find yourself in what looks like a subpar situation, think about how you can begin to put things in "motion" to create a turnaround.

> **Power Point Question**

How can "creating motion" better enable you to overcome?

"Be strong and do not give up, for your work will be rewarded."
—2 Chronicles 15:7 (NIV)

McDonald's heiress fills buckets

The Salvation Army received the largest single donation ever given to a charitable service organization. The gift of $1.5 billion, which will be used to build and maintain 25–30 community centers, came from the estate of Joan Kroc.

Mrs. Kroc made a very generous donation. Yet she is not the only super-wealthy person who has been generous with money. There are many others, such as **Bill Ford, Jr.**, CEO of Ford Motor Company, who gave his first bonus—worth about $1.5 million—to company employees for their children's college tuition.[1] Another example is **Bill Gates** and his wife, Melinda, who have given away $28.3 billion (or about 37 percent) of their total net worth.[2]

Why do these wealthy people give their money away?

According to multimillionaire **John Marks Templeton**, who was the founder of the Templeton Investment Fund, it is because "many of the world's most successful and influential people experience a greater reward in giving their wealth than in getting it. It is through giving, not getting, that one can exert a truly positive force for good. If one wants to get more out of life, they have to give more to life."[3]

But what if you do not have millions or billions to give away? Look at what some others are doing:

- "New Orleans Hornets forward **P. J. Brown** and his wife, Dee, took 80 underprivileged children shopping at Toys 'R' Us...and paid for the gifts."[4]

- "Green Bay Packers wide receiver **Donald Driver**, who grew up homeless, bestowed houses on two less-fortunate families, one in Green Bay and the other in his hometown of Houston."[5]

- "Los Angeles Lakers forward **Karl Malone** donated shoes to the victims of local wildfires and floods."[6]

- "Midwest radio personality **Rick Couri** has, for the past sixteen years, spent several days each year involved in community fundraising projects, including riding a roller coaster 542 times to raise over $40,000."[7]

Not only do you help others by giving, but you also bring a greater joy and sense of purpose to your own life. In the words of psychologist William James, "The only truly happy people that I know are those who have found a cause greater than themselves to live for."[8] Malone agrees, "Being able to make a difference to those less fortunate...is a real privilege."[9]

The secret is this: Develop plans and strategies for being a blessing to others. Templeton concurs, "If you want to be happy, strive to make someone else happy."[10]

Power Point Question

What actions can you take this week in order to be a greater blessing to others?

_____

"A generous [person] *will prosper."*
—Proverbs 11:25 (NIV)

Vegetarians becoming flexitarians

Many people are becoming part-time vegetarians. The American Dialect Society calls them "Flexitarians."

I believe in being a "flexitarian"—not just in terms of diet, but also as a mind-set for living.

Flexibility, or the willingness to adapt and change, is a key element for success in any arena of life. Noted author and playwright **George Bernard Shaw** stated, "Progress is impossible without change."[1]

Yet there is a challenge. Change, by itself, can be disastrous. Any successful endeavor must have some form of structure, or it leads to chaos and uncertainty. On the other side of the coin, structure without the attitude of change leads to stagnation and eventual death. Therefore, in every situation, one must find a balance between structure and flexibility.

With that understanding, here is the key to the successful utilization of the mind-set of change: Recognize that change is not a concept just to be ingrained into long-range planning. To be really effective, flexibility must be integrated into one's daily routine.

For instance, each day, I have plans, schedules, and/or appointments. My day has a preplanned flow to it, but I live my life ready to adjust or alter my plans as new opportunities appear or circumstances change. I realize, as I have often stated, that "God cannot effectively use—or bless—anyone who is not willing to be interrupted." This strategy allows me to continually be open to fresh input and to "seize" the best for any given day and for my life in general.

In the biblical story about the farmer Elisha, the flexibility mind-set is demonstrated. Because he had this perspective, he embraced a major career change. In the story, Elisha was in his field, plowing away. (I am sure that he had set a plan for how many furrows he would plow that day.) Then the prophet Elijah walked by and called him to join him. The Bible states, *"He left the oxen and ran after Elijah"* (1 Kings 19:20). Because he was willing to quickly change his actions, he was able to seize the opportunity!

Here are some keys that have helped me to be a "change maker":

1. STABILITY: I strive for stability, permanence, and structure. However, I recognize that only eternal things are really permanent.

2. ATTITUDE: I think of changes not as inconveniences but as new adventures.

3. READINESS: I live ready to change. **Henry Ford** once said, "Before everything else, getting ready is the secret of success."[2] Thinking of potential changes in advance, I develop action plans to deal with opportunities if they occur.

4. TIMING: Although one can alter one's path at almost any time, some moments are more favorable for doing so than others. I attempt to be sensitive to what's going on so that I can perceive the right timing to make changes.

5. RAPID RESPONSE: When an opportunity that demands change occurs, I move quickly. Speed is often the difference between success and a missed opportunity.

Determine to make yourself more flexible and ready for change. Remember, as **John H. Patterson** said, "Only fools and dead men don't change their minds. Fools won't. Dead men can't."[3]

Power Point Question

How well do you anticipate and/or adjust for changes?

"And he left the oxen and ran."
—1 Kings 19:20 (NKJV)

Doorman refuses to hail cab

A doorman at a luxury New York City hotel refused to get a taxi for a vacationing couple who were hotel guests. He told them to "take a hike."

The doorman's attitude may sound like the height of rudeness and insensitivity. Actually, he was being considerate. When the couple asked for a cab, he informed them that their destination was only two blocks away and that they could save both time and the cab fare by walking. The couple gave the doorman a good tip and took a nice stroll.

An occasional walk might benefit a person only a little, but regular exercise can have great benefits. "According to the Centers for Disease Control and Prevention (CDC), more than 60 percent of all Americans don't get enough exercise. About 25 percent don't exercise at all."[1]

"Exercise has been proven to help with weight management, improve skeletal-muscle strength and endurance, cardiopulmonary fitness, flexibility, and possibly improve your immune system and mental health. Exercising twice weekly has been shown to reduce the threat of strokes by 40 percent, coronary heart disease by 15 percent."[2]

THE MANY BENEFITS OF REGULAR EXERCISE

Years ago, **Dr. Kenneth Cooper** began an intensive study of exercise. He discovered that people who exercised regularly had physical and medical improvements. However, he also found that if a person's exercise program was directed toward only muscle building, the individual rarely achieved good physical fitness.

In his best-selling book *Aerobics*, he explained what made the difference: "The key to fitness is oxygen. In the body, the fuel is food, and the flame is oxygen. The body can store food, but it can't store oxygen. As one increases his oxygen capability, he increases his endurance and overall fitness."[3]

Dr. Cooper then created an exercise program that focused on this element. "Aerobics is that form of exercise which forces the body to consume increased amounts of oxygen and as such is the only form of exercise that benefits not just the skeletal muscles but the whole body."[4]

My mother was a person who believed in the benefits of regular exercise. When she was ninety years old, she would still swim thirty laps in her home association's pool three times a week. People could not believe her age as she drove around in her convertible so happy and healthy.

> **Power Point**
>
> "In the body, the fuel is food, and the flame is oxygen."
> —Dr. Kenneth Cooper

A good exercise program need not take a lot of time. "Three 10-minute bouts of activity can be as effective a cardiovascular workout as one 30-minute session," says **Dr. Edward Laskowski**, codirector of the Sports Medicine Center at the Mayo Clinic.[5] Add years to your life, and increase your vitality and alertness, by having a regular exercise regimen.

> **Power Point Question**

In what ways would your productivity and enjoyment of life increase if you were more physically fit?

"Beloved, I wish above all things that thou...be in health."
—3 John 2

Bill to scrap inspections is ok'd

Responding to the fact that all but thirteen states have done away with auto inspections, one state assembly voted 67–32 to make mandatory state auto inspections a thing of the past.

Discontinuing auto inspections might be okay. However, you had better have some kind of follow-up inspection system in place if you are going to be an effective leader who delegates.

In order to maximize your efficiency, there are times when you must have others assist you. They can do the tasks that would prevent you from spending time on your most important and/or desirable tasks. Failing to do so will cause you to be less effective and more stressed out.

When you delegate, "you will achieve more results than you ever thought possible. You will have more time for managerial activities. You will find yourself focusing on doing a few tasks very well rather than doing a lot of things poorly."[1]

Here are some of my favorite quotes on the subject of delegating:

"Every day, I ask myself, 'What am I doing that can be done by someone else?'"
—**John Maxwell**[2]

"My secret is that I get things out of my hands and into someone else's."
—**David Ingles**[3]

"Never do anything that someone else can do for you, as well or better."
—**Raymond Johnson**[4]

"When you start running out of time, pay someone to give you more."
—**Joyce Meyer**[5]

A good biblical example of a challenge to delegate can be found in the life of Moses. When his father-in-law, Jethro, saw him trying to serve as the sole judge for the Israelites and solve innumerable disputes and legal questions, he told him,

Both you and these people who are with you will surely wear yourselves out. For this thing is too much for you; you are not able to perform it by yourself....Moreover you shall select from all the people able men....Every great matter they shall bring to you, but every small matter they themselves shall judge. So it will be easier for you, for they will bear the burden with you.

(Exodus 18:18, 21–22 NKJV)

Moses heeded this advice. "[He] *chose able men...and made them heads over the people*" (Exodus 18:25 NKJV).

You, also, can heed the words of Jethro. Over the next few weeks, practice delegating more. However, be sure to set up inspection systems. Not having follow-up systems is where many achievers have gotten "burned" while attempting to delegate. As I said earlier, quoting from my *Time Increase* CD series, "People do what is inspected, not what is expected."

Power Point Question

How could better delegation and inspection improve productivity and reduce stress in your life?

"You are not able to perform it by yourself."
—Exodus 18:18 (NKJV)

Dead woman gets job back

A woman died while going to a hearing to fight her job dismissal. Authorities say the woman, who was revived by paramedics, has fully recovered and was reinstated to her job.

Many women experience a sense of "dying" at certain times in their lives—an emotional death. For example, when the youngest child goes off to college, gets married, or just moves out on his or her own, a mother may believe that her role of nurturing and mentoring has ended. She may feel directionless and empty. Some people respond to this vacuum by indulging in a life of new activities, as exemplified by the following poem:

In the dim and distant past
When life's tempo wasn't fast,
Grandma used to rock and knit,
Crochet, tat and baby-sit.
When the kids were in a jam,
They could always count on Gram.
In an age of gracious living,
Grandma was the gal for giving.

Grandma now is at the gym,
Exercising to keep slim.
She's off touring with the bunch,
Taking clients out to lunch.
Going north to ski or curl,
All her days are in a whirl.
Nothing seems to stop or block her,
Now that Grandma's off her rocker!
—Unknown

Others, however, are discovering a new source of joy and excitement by mentoring their grandchildren. Such is the case with **Arvella Schuller,** wife of **Dr. Robert Schuller,** who is the pastor of the Crystal Cathedral located in Southern California. Arvella produces the *Hour of Power* television program, handles all the family's personal finances, has a speaking career, and does volunteer work.

MAKING GRANDCHILDREN A PRIORITY

Yet despite her busy schedule, Arvella has chosen to make her family—especially her fifteen grandchildren—a priority. She says, "A changing world can be a hurting and lonely world unless we see ourselves as comforters, companions, and counselors of those we love."[1]

Arvella regularly schedules time to give undivided attention to each grandchild. If one has a special need, she will be there regardless of her busy schedule.[2]

> **Power Point**
>
> "In a time of changing roles, certain roles need to remain unchanged."
>
> —Arvella Schuller[4]

My friend Betty Southard coauthored a book entitled *The Grandmother Book.* In it, she states, "Kids need to know that there is someone, beyond their parents, who loves them in a very special way. A grandparent's love and understanding complements the love they get from their parents."[3]

Arvella believes that one of the most valuable things that grandparents can do is to release their love, knowledge, wisdom, experience, and prayers into the lives of the younger generation.

Even if you do not have children or grandchildren, there probably are young people around you who would greatly benefit from having some of your love and attention. Why not make a difference in someone's life?

Power Point Question

How can you adjust your priorities or schedule in order to better mentor and influence your grandchildren or others of the younger generation?

———————

"The aged women...may teach the young women."
—Titus 2:3–4

Saboteurs derail train

An Amtrak train jettisoned off a 30-foot-high bridge into a dry stream bed. Several cars plunged from the bridge at 50 mph, coming to rest lying sideways on the sandy bottom of the desert wash.

The removal of twenty-nine spikes from the tracks by saboteurs caused the train to crash. Likewise, with achievers, seemingly little things, such as poor personal work habits, can cause personal and professional derailment.

Best-selling author **Stephen Covey** believes that derailment can happen when one does not clearly distinguish the difference between what is important and what is urgent. He says, "The problem is that when urgency becomes the dominant factor in our lives, then importance is not. Urgency itself is not the problem. The problem is that we can get so caught up in doing, we do not stop and ask if what we are doing really needs to be done."[1]

Covey believes that "effective management is putting first things first. While leadership decides what the 'first things' are, it is management that puts them first, day-to-day, moment-by-moment. This requires one to operate by values rather than by impulse or the desire of a given moment."[2]

Here are some strategies that I have learned for staying on track:

STAYING ON TRACK

1. STAY FOCUSED: Momentum is achieved not in the switchyard of multiple choices but on a single track heading toward a predetermined destination.

2. WATCH THE DETAILS: Do you regularly check and inspect the small but important areas of your business and life? The removal of a few rail spikes can derail an entire train.

3. MAKE YOUR CARGO MORE VALUABLE: Don't just stay on track financially. Live a morally consistent life. Private victories lead to a life of public impact and influence.

> **Power Point**
>
> "Effective management is putting first things first."
> —Stephen Covey

4. WRITE A DAILY PLAN: Without a plan for each day, you can easily get distracted handling the seemingly urgent tasks rather than the most important ones. Write out or create in your computer a daily "To Do" list based on what is truly important.

5. MAINTAIN BALANCE: Give time and attention to all the important areas of your life: health, family, financial, intellectual, social, professional, and spiritual. If a train gets too far off balance, it will overturn. So will you.

6. REWARD YOURSELF: At the end of a specific task or assignment, reward yourself by doing or making something you enjoy.

7. MAINTAIN PROPER FUEL LEVELS: Eat properly, exercise regularly, and get enough sleep. Also, infuse your life with spiritual power. Spend time reading the Bible, praising and worshipping God, and/or engaging in personal meditation.

The desired outcome of a goal-oriented life is to arrive at one's desired destination as quickly and efficiently as possible. Implementing the above strategies can help you stay on track and avoid being derailed and ending up at the bottom of a ditch.

Power Point Question

What are you doing to prevent personal and professional derailment?

"Turn not from it [God's will] to the right hand or to the left, that thou mayest prosper whithersoever thou goest."
—Joshua 1:7

Ancient jewelry found near Dead Sea

Using metal detectors, Israeli archeologists discovered treasures, including jewelry, while excavating caves near the Dead Sea.

A Pittsburgh man was not searching in caves, and he did not have a metal detector, but when it seemed as if his life was dead in the water, old jewelry helped him to find a whole new direction for his life.

For several years, I spoke at seminars with **Dr. Edwin Louis Cole**. Ed, who is now deceased, was a master at reaching out and helping men with their unique challenges concerning sex, marriage, and money. At some of these seminars, he shared the story of this man, who had a whole new life emerge out of a negative event.

The man had worked at a steel mill for twenty-two years. Unexpectedly, the mill was shut down, and he found himself with no job, no retirement funds, and unemployment pay that was running out. As the days and weeks passed with no apparent solution, tension mounted within him, and the former steelworker became depressed and irritable. He started going for long walks to get out of the house and to occupy himself.

THE BEGINNING OF A NEW BUSINESS

One evening, a bad snowstorm hit the city. The next day, he went for his customary walk and noticed a neighbor looking out her window. Realizing that, because of the snow, she could not get out of her house, he stopped and offered to shovel the snow away from her doors and sidewalk. She offered to pay him, but he refused to take any money for his help.

The next day, another neighbor, who had seen the good job he had done, offered to pay him to shovel her sidewalk. Seeing a business opportunity, he used this money to buy shovels for both himself and his sons, who began to shovel snow for people after school. When spring came, the woman asked him if he would clean her backyard and attic. He took home some of the jewelry, appliances, and other things that she wanted him to discard. Then he cleaned and/or fixed them up and sold them.

Building upon this idea, he and his boys then started going from house to house asking people if they wanted their yards and attics cleaned. They made money on their labor and also obtained unusual things to sell.

> **Power Point**
>
> "God can create something out of things that seem like nothing."
> —Edwin Louis Cole

The man told Ed, "Soon I was operating a clean-up business plus an antiques store and was making more money than I ever had at the mill."

Ed concluded this story by sharing that the man told him, "Getting laid off was the best thing that ever happened to me."

Power Point Question

How can you more creatively react to negative events?

"I will give thee the...hidden riches of secret places."
—Isaiah 45:3

Globe littered with land mines

It is estimated that the world is littered with 80 to 100 million antipersonnel land mines spread over 64 different countries.

They may look harmless, but the ability of land mines to kill or maim is just a footstep away. The road to success is littered with mines. However, these mines are not buried in the ground. Instead, they can be found in the minds of those individuals who are threatened by change. They normally ignite and explode out of the mouths of their carriers in response to someone suggesting that there is a better way, a different method, another viewpoint, or a need to change.

Donald Trump believes that "life's losers get their sense of accomplishment and achievement from trying to stop others."[1]

In his book *Peak Performance Principles for High Achievers*, **John Noe** states that high achievers "must be willing to risk rejection from their peers. If you study the biographies of great people, you will discover that most of them were misunderstood, often by those closest to them."[2] He also says, "They struggled against overwhelming obstacles and labors in the face of sharp criticism."[3]

Here are words and opinions that some high achievers of the past had to face.

LAND MINES OF THE PAST

"Drill into the ground to try and find oil? You're crazy."
—Workers to Edwin L. Drake, 1859

"The 'telephone' has too many shortcomings to be seriously considered as a means of communication. The device is inherently of no value to us."
—Western Union executive memo, 1876

"Heavier-than-air flying machines are impossible."
—President, British Royal Society, 1895[4]

"I have determined that there is no market for talking pictures."
—Thomas Edison[5]

"I have traveled the length and breadth of this country and talked with the best people, and I can assure you that data processing is a fad that won't last out the year."
—Major publisher's book editor, 1957

"We don't like their sound...guitar music is on the way out."
—Recording company executive, rejecting the Beatles, 1962[6]

"You ain't going nowhere son. You ought to go back to driving a truck."
—Grand Old Opry Manager to Elvis Presley[7]

> **Power Point**
>
> "Great rewards come to those with the courage to step away from the pessimistic crowd."[8]
> —John Noe

I am not saying that achievers should listen only to those who agree with them. Constructive criticism and wise advice are extremely valuable and should always be sought after and highly treasured. However, we must insulate ourselves from the negative, can't-do-it individuals whom we may encounter on the road to success.

In the words of the ancient Chinese proverb, "Man who says it cannot be done should not interrupt man who is doing it."

Power Point Question

Are you letting other people's negative words and/or actions keep you from crossing your "field of dreams"?

"And they spread...a bad report."
—Numbers 13:32 (NIV)

Power Point #68

Contest officials search for God

A publisher's sweepstakes notice arrived at a Florida Assemblies of God church addressed to "A. God." It notified "him" that he was a finalist for the $11 million top prize.

Florence Littauer, along with her husband, Fred, conducts marriage seminars and teaches on personality types in church groups, conferences, and conventions nationwide. I have appeared on the same program with them at numerous conferences, and they are always a big hit. Florence's book *Personality Plus* is a classic among those who study personality differences.

Florence and Fred's lives changed when God came to their home. After their two brain-damaged sons died, they found themselves in a desperate search to find their way out of the misery. They wanted to find answers to the unanswered questions in their lives. Florence often shares the story when she speaks.

"We were achieving on the surface, but we were hurting underneath. Fred went to the library and started studying books on religion. We soon came to realize what our problem was. We needed a spiritual force in control of our lives.

"Before they died, I learned this principle of control through my two brain-damaged sons. Each one had been beautiful to look at—blond hair, dimpled chins, and bright blue eyes. They had eyes, but they could not see; ears, but they could not hear; feet, but they could not walk. They looked all right on the outside, but without a proper functioning brain, with no controlling mechanism, nothing worked right.

"I realized that we were a lot like those boys. We looked all right on the outside, but inside, nothing much was working right."

When Florence and Fred experienced a spiritual renewal in their lives, they received newfound peace and a sense of purpose. As they continued to study the Bible, they also developed a fresh awareness that not everyone was created by God to function alike. Each person was unique and different. This understanding of uniqueness caused Florence to launch her career of teaching people to recognize, appreciate, and build successful career teams using the personality differences of others.

> **Power Point**
>
> "Appreciate people's differences and build upon them."
> —Florence Littauer[3]

Florence maintains that to effectively lead, we must determine that we are not going to let people's differences be an irritation to us. Instead, each of us must learn to appreciate people's differences and build upon them. She teaches, "How people handle their differences with others will largely determine their level of success or failure."

Best-selling author **Steven Covey** agrees with this approach to life. He teaches, "Valuing the differences of others is the essence of synergy. The person who is truly effective has the humility and reverence to appreciate the rich resources available through interaction with the minds and hearts of other human beings. Those differences add to his knowledge and to his understanding of reality."[1] Steven continues, "Consider ways in which differences might be used as stepping-stones to alternative solutions."[2]

Power Point Question

How can you better use the unique talents, giftings, and opinions of others in your business or family?

"For the body is not one member, but many."
—1 Corinthians 12:14

Varmints stink up school

For over a month, school teachers and staff members have been grappling with a smelly problem in one of their buildings. The stench was apparently caused by skunks, who were releasing odors near a drainage system next to one of the classroom complexes.

The "stink posse" at a local elementary school has given up. Apparently, heating intake vents were carrying the skunks' foul smell to all parts of the building. Teachers and students complained of headaches and had difficulty concentrating. Skunk traps were set but were ineffective, so school officials have decided to hire professionals to combat the "stink invasion."

Skunks are not the only things that can stink up your life—negative friends and critical associates can, also. However, when these "stinky varmints" start hanging around, they can cause more than headaches and loss of concentration. They can cause you to experience isolation and hostility.

Dr. Phil McGraw is a best-selling author and television personality. He believes that when people are continually exposed to negative input, they will begin to "choose thoughts that depreciate and demean themselves. They also choose the consequences of low self-esteem and low self-confidence...which are alienation and hostility."[1]

In addition, over time, their "internal dialogue" becomes negative. Dr. Phil defines internal dialogue as the "real-time conversations that you have with yourself about everything that is going on in your life." He believes that "regular exposure to negative internal dialogue, like prolonged exposure to the sun, can over time literally kill a person without them even knowing it. The reason is that they have created for themselves a toxic internal environment."[2]

If negative friends are stinking up your life, you have three options: (1) Choose to continue the relationship and suffer the consequences, (2) try to change their thinking, or (3) separate yourself from, or at least reduce your exposure to, their influence.

The choosing of one's inner circle of friends is one of the most important of all success strategies. Here are what some of my friends and fellow teachers say about those who influence the way we think about ourselves.

THE INFLUENCE OF FRIENDS

"It is not your accomplishments that will make you great, it's who you choose to surround yourself with."
—**General Norman Schwarzkopf**, USA, Retired[3]

"My choice to change my closest friends was a turning point in my life."
—**John Mason**, best-selling author of *An Enemy Called Average*[4]

> **Power Point**
>
> "Regular exposure to negative internal dialogue...can...kill a person."
> —Dr. Phil McGraw

"To increase, a person must find friends who have strengths they do not possess."
—**Mark Victor Hansen**, best-selling author of *Chicken Soup for the Soul*[5]

"To be a winner you must associate with winners."
—**Dexter Yager**, marketing crown distributor[6]

"Eaglelike folks may be rare, but they possess an incredible loyalty when they link up." —**Charles Swindoll**, radio personality and author[7]

"True friends are the ones who will be faithful and will keep you in touch with reality." —**Colin Powell**, former secretary of state[8]

"Success comes not from what you know but who you know."
—**Lee Iacocca**, former president of Chrysler Corporation[9]

Make a decision today to carefully choose those whom you surround yourself with.

Power Point Question

Do you have friends who are stinking up your life?

_____

"The companion of fools will suffer harm."
—Proverbs 13:20 (NASB)

Chic-fil-A wins quality award

The Atlanta-based company took top honors as "Best Drive-Thru in America."

Q SR magazine, a publication for restaurant owner-operators, awarded the restaurant chain for its excellence of operations. The study measured speed, accuracy, menu-board appearance, and speaker clarity.

Back in 1960, **Truett Cathy** never dreamed that one day he would be operating one of America's largest and most successful fast-food companies. On the contrary, he was facing one of his greatest crises. His second restaurant, The Dwarf House, had burned down. It seemed that his dreams for a successful career in food services had literally gone up in smoke. To make matters worse, that same week, doctors found cancerous polyps in his colon.

These bad circumstances could not stop him, however. He had confidence in himself and his God.

Truett quickly dealt with, and was able to overcome, his health problems. Soon he was rebuilding the restaurant. Only this time he made it different. He decided to open it as Atlanta's first self-serve fast-food restaurant specializing in chicken.

Sales were mediocre until he made a discovery. By removing the bone and skin from the chicken breast, he could cut the cooking time in half. This would greatly decrease his expenses. He then came up with the idea of putting the breast on a bun and adding special seasonings. The Chick-fil-A sandwich was born, and the rest is history. Today, even though every store is closed on Sundays, the more than 1,100 Chick-fil-A outlets across America bring in some of the industry's top sales income per unit.[1]

I had the opportunity to visit with Mr. Cathy in Washington, D.C. He is a happy and gracious man who is very involved with various charities. He shared with me some of the reasons why he believes that "it is easier to succeed than to fail":

It Is Easier to Succeed Than to Fail

- "It's easier to succeed because success eliminates the agony and frustration of defeat."

- "It's easier to succeed because money spent to fail must be spent again to succeed."

- "It's easier to succeed because feelings of discouragement and discontent accompany failure, but joy and excitement come from succeeding."[2]

> **Power Point**
>
> "Fifty percent of the battle ends when you make up your mind."
> —S. Truett Cathy[7]

Mr. Cathy succeeded because he would not let a setback stop him from pursuing his dreams. **Robert Schuller** concurs with this attitude. He says, "There are black holes surrounding all of us."[3] However, true achievers "are empowered by problems. These people turn every problem into a decision...a decision to overcome."[4]

My friend **Myles Munroe** states, "All leaders, regardless of their abilities...will encounter crises....A crisis is...simply a turning point at which leadership ability is tested and matured. A crisis can lead you to greater challenge and victory."[5]

Do you have problems that need to be turned into victories? If so, go for it. In the words of Robert Schuller, "It is better to attempt to do something great and fail than to do nothing and succeed."[6]

Power Point Question

Is there some change in attitude, methods, or techniques that could bring you increase?

"My yoke is easy, and my burden is light."
—Matthew 11:30

$200,000 paid for lunch

A Singapore businessman bid $202,000 on eBay for the opportunity to have a private lunch with financial legend Warren Buffet.

People are willing to pay large sums of money for a seat if they believe that it provides them with a special opportunity to make money, gain prestige, and/or experience great enjoyment.

For instance, in the financial arena, not long ago, a seat on the New York Stock Exchange sold for $2.6 million.[1] In the political arena, during the Clinton presidency, it was reported that a seat at the dinner table for a special occasion at the White House could be arranged for those who made a $100,000 donation to "the party."[2]

In the business arena, because of the perceived value of the material being taught, I have known people to pay up to $7,500 for a seat at a three-day success seminar. In the athletic realm, I was speaking in Atlanta while the World Series was being played there, and I heard that because of the people's enthusiasm for the team, the available seats were selling for $1,000 each.

Sometimes, however, a "special seat" becomes available because of reasons other than money. I have experienced several of these occasions in my life. Because of my friendships and speaking venues, I have had the wonderful opportunity to dine, fellowship, and share with some great people such as Margaret Thatcher, George H. W. Bush, Mikhail Gorbachev, Colin Powell, Dr. Robert Schuller, Larry King, Bob Costas, Loretta Scott King, Rudolph Giuliani, Bob Dole, and others.

When these opportunities occur, I make it a point to maximize the experience. Here are some things I have learned about such opportunities that can help to increase your enjoyment and personal impact when you encounter them.

MAXIMIZING ENCOUNTERS WITH WELL-KNOWN PEOPLE

1. PREPARE IN ADVANCE: Study and obtain background information about key VIPs. Think about, and maybe even make notes of, questions to ask during conversations that will better enable you to relax and cherish the experience as well as carry on intelligent dialogue.

> **Power Point**
>
> "Most celebrities love to associate with 'real' people."
> —Bob Harrison

2. BE YOURSELF: Most celebrities love to associate with "real" people who are enjoyable to be around.

3. SHOW INTEREST: Maintain focus, show a caring attitude, and be interested in them and what they are sharing.

4. TALK MINIMALLY: Concentrate your conversation on friendly chat—asking for knowledge and/or discovering common points of interest.

5. BE TIME CONSCIOUS: Leaders are normally on tight schedules. They will relax and better enjoy their visit with you if they sense that you respect their time.

6. CAPTURE THE MOMENT: In order to relive the memory of the occasion, obtain a program, pictures, or autographs.

7. BE THANKFUL: Send a note of appreciation to the host(s).

> **Power Point Question**

Which of the above keys can you activate to increase the impact and memories of your special opportunities?

_____

"Mary has chosen what is better [sitting and visiting with Jesus]*."*
—Luke 10:42 (NIV)

Many still in the dark

The storm that swept through the state has left 50,000 residents without power and in the dark.

One day **James Stovall** found himself in the dark. It was not because of a power failure; he had gone blind. The degenerative eye disease that doctors had discovered when he was seventeen had finally taken its toll.

Stovall moved into a nine-by-twelve-foot room in the back of his home, having no idea what he would do with the rest of his life. He exclaims, "My whole world had shrunk to that little room. However, after months in that room, I asked myself, 'What is the worst thing that can happen to me if I leave this room?'...None of them seemed as bad as spending the rest of my life there."[1]

That day he walked fifty feet to his mailbox. There has been no stopping him since. As founder of the Narrative Television Network, every year he produces narrated versions of over one thousand movies and television shows. In addition, he speaks at large events three times a month and has authored twelve books.

At one of my Increase Events, he shared, "I awoke one morning and found that I could not see. Since then, I have discovered that there is a second blindness that many people have. It has nothing to do with a physical problem. It has to do with the fact that most people lack the ability to make any sense out of their lives—to become the people they were created to be."

"Sight is a function of the eyes; vision is a function of the heart."[2] So says my friend and fellow teacher **Myles Munroe**. "[Nothing great] was ever done without...this mysterious force called vision....Vision generates hope in the midst of despair and provides endurance in tribulation....Without vision, life would be a study in cyclic frustration within a whirlwind of despair. Vision is the foundation of courage."[3]

Munroe continues, saying, "Your future is not ahead of you—it lies within you...vision determines your destiny,"[4] and "Vision is the juice of life. It is the prerequisite for passion and the source of persistence. When you have vision, you know how to stay in the race and complete it."[5]

Stovall says, "I may have lost my sight, but in the aftermath, I gained a greater vision than I ever had before. I choose not to let blindness squelch my ambition...or the pursuit of my personal destiny. I may have lost my sight, but I have gained greater vision than I ever had before. Going blind was the best thing that ever happened to me."[6]

> **Power Point**
>
> "What appears to be the ending can be the point of a new beginning."
> —James Stovall

Power Point Question

Do you have a vision for your life?

"Then the eyes of the blind shall be opened."
—Isaiah 35:5

Elevator suddenly plunges

An elevator that was overloaded with 17 prisoners and 2 deputies suddenly took a two-story plunge. When one of the guards got in and closed the door, authorities reported that "the ride from hell started."

When I read the story about the elevator plunging, I recalled occasions some time ago when different sales achievers came to me in desperation because their incomes had unexpectedly taken a "plunge." It was out of those experiences that I began to teach people and companies strategies on how to have a more stable base of income by creating customer loyalty. One key way that this is achieved is by maintaining contact with customers in order to get referrals and repeat business.

Years later, I had the opportunity to meet a man who was a master at marketing. **Ken Kerr**, who has since passed away, and I became friends and often exchanged ideas. He was the creative project director for Walt Disney's Epcot Center. In addition, he developed marketing programs for Sea World and several other corporations.

SUCCESSFUL MARKETING THROUGH REPEAT SALES

Ken believed that the most successful marketing strategies consisted of developing products and programs for repeat sales. He shared the following story on the value of repeat sales at one of my Hawaii Increase Events:

"One of my clients ran a promotion to sell a collection of coins to new customers for $19. He actually lost a few dollars on every sale. Over 50,000 people responded to the offer.

"The next month, he sent out a follow-up mailing to all those who had purchased the $19-dollar item. Nearly 10,000 of those same people bought an 'after-sale' collection at $1,000 each. My client made a $2 million profit on the after-sale.

"Not only that, but three months later, he again solicited the original 50,000 people who had bought the $19 coin sets. About 250 of them bought the $1,000 collection. That made him another $50,000 in profits.

"That's not all. Later, he contacted those 10,000 people who had purchased the after-sale $1,000 collection and gave them an additional offer. About 1,500 of them bought more coins, averaging $5,000 per order. This made him another $500,000.

> **Power Point**
>
> "It is what comes after the original sale that matters most."
>
> —Ken Kerr

"There's still more. Many of the customers continued ordering coins and collections from him for some time, creating extra income every year. All this from an original promotion that began with a $19-dollar offer."

Ken also shared the following statistics regarding repeat sales:

- Years ago, Home Depot found that its typical customer spent an average of $38 per sale. However, based upon a lifetime of repeat sales with the same customer, the total amount per customer could soar to $25,000.

- Continental Airlines discovered that the long-term economic value of a customer standing before a ticket agent could be as much as one hundred times the amount of that day's ticket transaction.

According to Ken, the secret is this: "Never look at customers in terms of one-time sales. Go back to them for repeat business. In sales, "It is what comes after the original sale that matters most."

Tom Peters, one of America's top success authorities, also teaches salespeople this concept. He tells them to "consider every customer to be a potential lifelong relationship, generating word-of-mouth references as well as future business."[1]

> **Power Point Question**

Do you have additional products and/or services that you could offer your new or existing customers?

"Other seed fell on good soil, where it produced a crop—a hundred, sixty or thirty times what was sown."
—Matthew 13:8 (NIV)

Ugly lamp brings small fortune

A Florida man is thinking about all the ways he can spend the money that lamp fetched at an auction—$35,200!

The man in the above story never gave much thought to a small lamp that he had purchased years earlier. The auctioneer called it "an ugly little lamp," but someone else placed a high value on it and purchased it for this seemingly unbelievable price. His desire for the lamp was so great that he was willing to "pay the price."

When I read this article, I was reminded of a story shared by **Gary Richardson** at one of my Increase Events. Because he won the largest legal judgment in state history—$58 million—Gary is referred to as the "Top Gun of Oklahoma Attorneys." The story was about an incident that took place between Gary and one of his sons several years ago, and it addresses the issue of being willing to pay the price.

ARE YOU WILLING TO PAY THE PRICE?

Gary's son, Chuck, was a first-year student at Baylor University in Waco, Texas, at the time. One day, he called his dad and told him that he was planning to drop a math course before an upcoming big exam. He proceeded to tell Gary all the reasons why the course was too difficult and why he was not able to complete it.

Gary asked him to wait on making the decision and suggested that they meet in Dallas to discuss it over dinner the next night.

Gary drove to Dallas and, at dinner, told his son that he wasn't being honest with himself about what the issue really was. He stated, "You may have to study thirty, fifty, or seventy hours this weekend to do well. But you are smart, and if you put in the study time, you can pass the exam. The issue is not ability. It's simply this: Are you willing to pay the price?

Gary continued, "Another thing, Son. All your life, you'll be faced with similar challenges. How you react to these challenges will develop a pattern in your life that will say either 'I will meet the challenge with God's help' or 'I will cut and run.' This decision could be the beginning of your developing either one of these patterns. Which one do you desire? The decision is yours."

Gary's son decided to stay in the course. He had to spend the entire weekend studying. The following Tuesday, he took the test and made the top grade in the class. Not only that, but he has also developed the habit of overcoming adversity. He is the former Tulsa County District Attorney and is now practicing law with his dad.

> **Power Point**
>
> "You must have unwavering faith that you can prevail."
> —Jim Collins[2]

The belief in one's mastery to meet challenges as they arrive is called self-efficacy. Stanford psychologist Albert Bandura states that "people who have developed a strong self-efficacy approach problems in terms of how to handle them rather than worrying about what can go wrong."[1]

When facing adversity, each decision you make helps to form your habit patterns, which, in turn, will determine your destiny.

Power Point Question

What challenge in your life are you dealing with that can help set a habit pattern of overcoming?

_____

"We are well able to overcome."
—Numbers 13:30

Movie star makes deathbed confessions

An actor was deeply hurt that his three children from previous marriages refused to visit him on his deathbed.

It was reported that the 67-year-old star, who died in the arms of his fourth wife, was racked with shame and guilt as he apologized for the way he had lived his life.

How do you want to be remembered? **Stephen Covey** believes that it helps people's inner guidance systems if they take a few minutes to contemplate their own funerals. He says, "What would you want each of the speakers to say about you and your life? What character would you want them to have seen in you? What contributions and achievements would you want them to remember?"[1]

I believe that one of the most important things to be remembered for is a life marked by exemplary character. This kind of life becomes a role model for others, especially one's own children.

Such was the life of my father, **Dr. Irvine Harrison**.

Dad was a decisive leader who had the ability to persevere and win. Besides being immensely successful, having earned two doctorates, serving as the president of a college, and enjoying achievements in many different arenas, my father lived a life based upon principles. Dad was a man of wisdom, love, forgiveness, and integrity. He did not just read the Bible, but he also did his best to live it.

When he died, I stood behind the casket at his funeral to address the hundreds who had gathered there from across the nation, and I was so grateful to be the son of a man of such positive character. That day, my eulogy contained the following prose.

What Do I Tell You about Dad after He Is Gone?

Do I tell you about my feelings for my father?

That I loved him and respected him, that I will miss him?

Do I tell you about our great family experiences?

How he invested in his children by including them in many trips and outings?

Do I tell you about his concern for his son's future?

How he gave caring advice and financial support for my education and career?

Do I tell you about his life of character and integrity?

That I never heard him tell a lie nor saw him cheat anyone?

> **Power Point**
>
> "What do you want to be remembered for?"
>
> —St. Augustine

I shared about how I believed that the most important things that a parent can leave behind are not money and inheritances but positive memories and an exemplary life example.

I concluded my sharing that day by stating that my dad died on my 29th birthday. For my present that year, I received an incredible heritage: a memory of a man of stability who loved his family, had faith in God, and daily lived a life of character. These memories have inspired me and guided me throughout my life.

Power Point Question

What do you want to be remembered for?

_____

"The just man walketh in his integrity: his children are blessed after him."
—Proverbs 20:7

Student honesty linked to discounts

University students now get a discount card good at local shops if they sign a pledge not to cheat.

Honesty did not give my friend **George Reece** discounts at stores. However, it did provide him with the opportunity to become a partner in a development firm.

As a young carpenter, George started his career of building homes. He operated his own construction business for several years. Then a large home-building firm noticed his superior work ethic and the quality of his projects. They hired him to become one of their foremen. Because he was faithful, hardworking, and performed well, he received several promotions.

One day, the two senior partners of the company asked George to meet with them. As they were sitting in a secluded area of a restaurant, they started asking him questions about his work and job. Finally, one of them leaned forward and asked, "George, if it was necessary, for the good of the company, would you lie for us?"

George's thoughts raced: *If I don't answer correctly, here goes my opportunity with this firm.* He pondered. Would he be willing to lie for them? He knew that answering yes might be the only way to keep his job and get the promotion he desired.

A FOUNDATION OF INTEGRITY

After a brief pause, George took courage and confidently stated, "I'm sorry, but I could not lie for you." The senior partner leaned back, gave a sigh of relief, and said, "That is the right answer because we know that if you won't lie for us then you won't lie to us. We want to offer you a position as a partner in the firm."

For George, that one decision not to compromise his integrity opened up a whole new dimension of living for him. As Managing Partner of a development company that does over $200 million of income a year, he travels on a private jet. He is enjoying life with his wife and family, has three homes, and is a generous giver to his church and charities. All this happened because he made being honest a foundational strategy of his life.

William F. James, founder of Boys Town of Missouri, said, "There are really only three things necessary for success: first, normal intelligence; second, determination; and third, absolute honesty. One cannot be a little dishonest—it is all the way or nothing."[1]

> ### Power Point
>
> "Honesty is the single most important factor having a direct bearing on... success."
> —Ed McMahon[2]

Power Point Question

How would you have responded to the question about lying?

"They that deal truly are [the LORD'S] *delight."*
—Proverbs 12:22

Sheriff is resident of jail he built

A law officer is in jail after pleading no contest to six felony counts for filing false travel claims.

When he was in office, the sheriff fought for years to build a new jail for the county. Now, he has become a resident of that jail.

It is one thing to be in jail because you committed a crime. However, what if you were in jail and did not need to be?

Author **Lou Tice**, president of the Pacific Institute in Seattle, Washington, shares such an incident in his book *Smart Talk*. "Imagine yourself imprisoned. Then someone comes along and tells you, 'You imprisoned yourself. You chose to be your own judge and jury. You sentenced yourself to a life of poverty, or mediocrity, or to being an ineffective person. You do not need to stay in jail. The key to the cell door is in your pocket. You can unlock it and walk out free.'"[1]

Tice is referring to people who are imprisoned by their thinking, people who believe that their current reality is fixed. A person's beliefs can literally determine the limitations that they accept and live with.

Best-selling author **Suze Orman** refers to this limiting mind-set, stating, "The road to financial freedom begins not in a bank or even in your financial planner's office. It begins in your head—your thoughts."[2]

Several years ago, **Tim Flynn**, one of my closest friends, made a decision to "unlock" his limiting beliefs and experience a whole new life. When I challenged Tim to plan a "mental breakout," he was making just $15,000 per year. Soon thereafter, he personally made $3.5 million—in one day. Now he operates several businesses, is positively impacting our generation, and is mentoring others on how to enjoy all that God intends for them.

Here are some of Tim Flynn's success strategies:

WINNING POINTERS

1. PRIORITIZE: 20 percent of your work will produce 80 percent of the results. Do more of the 20 percent.

2. INTEGRITY: Require yourself and your staff to operate at the highest level of honesty and integrity.

3. QUALITY: Reputation, based upon how you perform your jobs, is one of your best forms of advertising.

4. FRIENDSHIP: Surround yourself with people of excellence and character.

5. TIMING: Learn to "read" the rhythms of your customers and the marketplace.

> **Power Point**
>
> "True success is...
> the ability...
> to sustain."
> —Tim Flynn

6. THINK LONG-TERM: True success is not the ability to obtain, but to sustain.

7. HELP OTHERS: God gave you a past so that you could help give others a future.

If you feel trapped by limiting beliefs, stop making excuses and organize a "breakout." As Tim says, "While losers are trying to explain the waves in the storm that sunk them, champions are building a new ship."

> **Power Point Question**

Do you have limiting beliefs that are holding you captive?

"A wise man will hear, and will increase learning."
—Proverbs 1:5

Bush parachutes for his 80th birthday

Former president George H. W. Bush celebrated his 80th birthday by parachuting to his presidential library.

R eading the article about former president **George H. W. Bush** parachuting onto the grounds of his presidential library on his birthday reminded me of a time some friends and I had with him at a luncheon in Tampa, Florida. During our time together, he was asked what he perceived to be the most difficult problem facing the United States today. Bush replied, "The most serious problem facing America is the decline of the traditional family."

I personally believe that one of the things that has caused this decline is that so many couples get too busy. Figuratively, they only parachute into each other's lives for meals, social events, and occasional romance. Over time, the closeness and intimacy that they once shared fades away like paint on a sun-scorched building.

Yet, when most achievers come to the sunset years of their lives, it is not their careers but rather their spouses and children that matter most to them. For instance, **Admiral Richard Byrd** wrote on his deathbed, "At the end the only thing that really matters is family. Anything and everything else is insubstantial."[1]

Billy Graham once said, "I made a big mistake. I left my family too much. If I could do it again, I would spend more time with them."[2]

Zig Ziglar believes that the secret to longevity of marriage is this: "Believe that love and romance will be alive as long as the marriage exists—and that the marriage will exist as long as you do."[3] Former president **Jimmy Carter** concurs, "My first loyalty is and will always be family."[4]

Best-selling author **Gary Smalley** believes that the main ingredient for a loving and lasting marriage is honor. He states, "Honor basically means to attach a high value, worth, or importance to a person. If your spouse feels less important than your vocation or activities, then you are not honoring him or her as the most important person in your life. My wife is worth more to me than anything on this earth...and she knows it."[5]

Arvella Schuller believes that this mind-set is a key to the strength and happiness of her marriage to **Dr. Robert Schuller**: "Our slogan is that together we are a great team."[6]

Great marriages and families don't just happen. It takes commitment, understanding, and patience. However, the benefits are well worth the effort.

If you are not experiencing the relationship that you desire, do what best-selling author **Randy Gibbs** recommends: "Decide what each of you must be and do in order to have what you want."[7]

> **Power Point**
>
> "The most serious problem facing America is the decline of the traditional family."
> —George H. W. Bush

Power Point Question

How can you improve your relationship with your spouse?

"Submitting yourselves one to another."
—Ephesians 5:21

Arab sheik buys 40 college degrees

A rich oil baron who cannot read or write has received more than 40 college degrees, six of them doctorates.

The receiving of college diplomas, medals, awards, or citations is very important to some people. Not only do such honors furnish an element of personal pride and recognition, but they also often cause a future increase in income in the marketplace.

Because of the power and prestige that is attached to earning money or being honored with degrees and awards, people will often put forth extraordinary effort to receive them. This sheik got his degrees from a university in his hometown—that he built. Since one of my daughters, **Wendy Joy Murakami**, did not own a university, she had to be more creative to receive an award that she greatly desired.

Wendy has always been a determined, bright, and innovative person. At university, she was able to maintain academic excellence even though she traveled with me to several overseas meetings and assisted at many of my Increase Events.

For her senior project, she led a team that did a masterful job of analyzing a local business and coming up with creative ways to increase its sales and profits. In fact, the report of the results of their project was so good that it was declared the best senior paper by the school of business. The university even submitted it for state competition.

Wendy was ecstatic about this honor, which showcased her superior marketing and management skills. Then she discovered that no formal recognition or award was given by the school of business for having the best senior project. Since the school gave recognition to other academic accomplishments, and since this project was such a major undertaking, she could not understand why it was not treated similarly.

The Rewards of Innovation and Determination

Instead of accepting this "non-recognition status quo," she began the process of trying to get the recognition for the team that she believed the task merited. She talked to her teacher and the department chairman and pushed through the various academic channels until an idea was born. She prepared a proposal for the business school to offer a Best Senior Paper Award to be presented each year as part of the awards presentations that took place during the hooding ceremonies on graduation weekend. She even sent along a sample award that she had prepared on her computer.

The dean responded, "It's never been done before, but why not?"

A few weeks later, on graduation weekend, our family attended the hooding ceremony. Several students received academic and merit awards. Many parents radiated with pride at the accomplishments of their offspring. However, none could have been any prouder than I was. My daughter not only received an award, but she also had the innovativeness and determination to create the award—for her team, herself, and all the recipients who would come after them in the future.

> **Power Point**
>
> "When a powerful hunger for your dreams is driving you...the ideas will come."
> —Les Brown[1]

Power Point Question

What has it cost you not to pursue harder what you know to be worthwhile goals and dreams?

"I pursue what is good."
—Psalm 38:20 (NIV)

Jet crashes short of runway

"Mayday! Mayday! We're going down!" was the urgent message the pilot sent out shortly before the airliner crashed.

According to investigators, while the crew had been concentrating on solving a landing gear problem, they had failed to notice the severity of a different developing problem: The plane was running out of fuel. The plane crashed and 174 of the passengers miraculously survived.

This is not an isolated example. According to *USA Today*, over one nine-year period, 39 passenger planes left the gate or took off without enough fuel.[1]

Running out of fuel is a problem that many achievers also face. They start on their flight to success only to discover that they don't have sufficient "fuel" to finish the course, and they suddenly drop out of sight.

During a seminar in Little Rock, Arkansas, I was visiting backstage with **Tom Hopkins**, one of the world's top sales trainers. He made a profound statement concerning success: "The single most important ingredient to success is the ability to last."

Shortly thereafter, I was talking with a friend who had just spent time with one of the world's premier religious leaders. My friend asked the minister what, more than anything else, was his secret to his achieving such great long-term success. The leader replied, "I lasted."

If you desire to achieve continuing success, it is critical that you have enough energy, resources, and motivation to finish the course.

THE FUELING EDGE

There are several things that you can do to stay "fueled up."

1. MAKE A DREAM LIST: List ten things that you want to achieve, have, and/or give. Regularly envision and talk about these items so that you can "touch" them.

2. ASSOCIATE WITH SUCCESSFUL PEOPLE: Pick up their attitudes and habits. Discover their success secrets. Learn to feel comfortable in their environment.

3. LISTEN TO MOTIVATIONAL AND TEACHING CDs/TAPES: Repetition is the best way to get new truths embedded into your subconscious.

4. MAKE POSITIVE CONFIRMATIONS: Your world is framed by your words. Talk about your desired destinations.

5. READ MIND-EXPANDING BOOKS: Empower and motivate yourself. Learn how others activate success strategies.

6. TAKE TIME FOR ENJOYMENT: Balance work and leisure. See time away from work as a season of refreshing and empowerment. Schedule good times—whether it is engaging in a hobby, driving a "fun" car, or visiting a favorite site.

> **Power Point**
>
> "The single most important ingredient to success is the ability to last."
> —Tom Hopkins

7. IDENTIFY POSSIBLE FUEL LEAKS: Discover and then either reduce or eliminate those things that drain you of productive energy and creativity.

8. SUSTAIN SPIRITUAL STRENGTH: Through regular devotions, meditation, and prayer, keep your "inner man" strong.

As author **Herbert Freudenberger** states in his book *Burn Out,* "The more well rounded out your life is, the more protected you are against burn out."[2]

Power Point Question

What are you doing to maintain your "fueling edge"?

"Let us run with patience the race that is set before us."
—Hebrews 12:1

Wife victimized by chiseling Romeo

After her husband left her, the woman discovered that he had stolen $50,000 through forged documents and unauthorized credit card purchases.

They met in the summer. Several weeks later, they flew to Reno and were married. Police said the wife never saw any of her husband's identification cards or licenses and now believes his name was an alias.

As foolish as it may seem for this lady to have married someone she hardly knew, it is not uncommon for a variation of this scenario to transpire in the marketplace. It occurs when people who do not know each other well come together for a project or large financial transaction. As in the above story, the outcome of the relationship is often disastrous.

James Guinn, who is a CPA, noted author, and seminar speaker from Dallas, Texas, cautions people particularly concerning their investments. Jim's firm specializes in advising major ministries and charities. I have visited with him at numerous board meetings and have had the opportunity to glean from his many years of experience.

The following are some of his warnings of possible risky investments, along with my thoughts on them.[1]

DON'T BE THE NEXT VICTIM

1. SOUNDS TOO GOOD: "If the investment sounds unbelievable or unreal, then it probably is." Safe investments seldom offer exorbitant rates of return. A projected high return on an investment causes me to investigate more thoroughly.

2. MUST BE KEPT CONFIDENTIAL: "If, because of the secretive nature of the investment, the promoter discourages you from talking

to your financial advisor, CPA, or attorney, be cautious." Most of the millionaires that I know never get involved in any major financial transaction without seeking counsel and advice from trusted aides and advisors.

3. HAS NO TRACK RECORD: "Always insist on receiving verifiable references from associates and/or previous investors. If these are not available, then it is probably best that you don't invest." Even if the person is of good character, he might not have the experience to prudently handle your money. As my friend **Myles Munroe** says, "Do not trust a person without a history."[2]

4. REQUIRES CASH BEFORE DISCLOSURE: "If the promoter requires cash before furnishing you all the details, be very cautious." Get all the information that you desire or do not hand over the cash that the promoter wants.

5. IT'S NOW OR NEVER: "If the promoter tries to rush you to invest because the investment opportunity is limited and 'going fast,' be very careful." I have personally always made it a policy that I would rather miss a potentially good opportunity than make a big mistake.

When considering major investments, the most important strategy is this: Be cautious and wise. As noted speaker **Marilyn Hickey** says, "You can have a lot of money, but if you don't have wisdom, you can kiss the money goodbye."[3]

Power Point Question

What strategies do you have in place to prevent yourself from making bad investments?

"A malicious man disguises himself with his lips."
—Proverbs 26:24 (NIV)

Bird causes power outage at airport

Los Angeles International Airport suffered a power outage when a bird landed on a power line causing a blackout and delaying flights for 1½ hours.

Dennis Byrd experienced a "power outage," but it was caused by a collision with a teammate in a football game. The New York Jets defensive end lay flat on his back on the artificial surface of Giants Stadium. All he needed to do was push himself up off the grass, as he had done a thousand times before, and get up. When he tried to move, however, he felt something give way. He heard it, too—a grinding and crunching at the top of his spine. He did not have the power to move his legs. Ten minutes later, he was carted off the field, put into an ambulance, and rushed to the hospital.[1]

Later, it was determined that the collision had broken his neck and left him paralyzed from the waist down.

During the next few months, Dennis had to fight physically, mentally, and spiritually, believing that he would walk again. Dennis' body functions began to improve at what the medical staff told him was an amazing rate. His muscular strength and control got better every day. Soon, he could walk without even limping, bench over 100 pounds, and lift 250 pounds on the leg sled.

In his book *Rise and Walk*, Dennis shared what he believed were the three main forces that enabled him to overcome this tragedy.

WINNING AGAINST ADVERSITY

1. DETERMINATION: "I used determination every minute that I was in the hospital and rehab rooms....Never give up is a lesson that I had learned on the football field."

Jack Canfield, coauthor of the best-selling book *Chicken Soup for the Soul,* believes that having the right attitude is a key to winning in any area of life. He states, "Attitude has a lot to do with a person's success and their ability to get what they want."[2]

2. LOVE OF FAMILY: According to best-selling author and authority on successful marriages, **Gary Smalley**, "Genuine love is far more than feeling. It means a commitment to care for and love your spouse unconditionally...no matter what happens."[3] Dennis shares from his personal life, "My wife and children were beside me encouraging me when it counted most."

> **Power Point**
>
> "It is not whether you get knocked down but whether or not you get back up."
> —Vince Lombardi[6]

3. FAITH IN GOD: A survey of doctors by the American Academy of Family Physicians found that "99 percent of the doctors believe there is an important relationship between spirit and flesh."[4] Dennis stated, "Knowing that God is with us even when we are down can help to make us whole. I had an awareness of the presence of God undergirding me and giving me the power to bounce back."[5]

Although his football-playing days are now over, Dennis is living a vibrant and happy life sharing with people that they can overcome and win against most any adversity.

Power Point Question

If you could hear God whispering to you, "I am with you," would you give up?

"I will never leave you nor forsake you."
—Joshua 1:5 (NIV)

Man trapped in outhouse overnight

A man was rescued after spending a hot summer night trapped in an outhouse.

This man's dilemma occurred when the structure's wooden handle accidentally dropped, trapping him inside. According to authorities, he "was unhurt but in a pretty foul mood."

Pioneering heart transplant surgeon **Dr. Christian Bernard** claimed that the greatest progress in health care in the last five hundred years came not from a drug or surgical procedure, but from the invention of the flushing toilet. The reason is that it provided a means to get rid of waste and thus eliminated many of the plagues that were caused by contaminated water supplies.[1]

The ability to get rid of waste effectively is a key to success in any arena of life. For the achiever, this is particularly true when dealing with time.

Time management expert **Edwin Feldman** stated, "Just as there are ways not to get things done, there are also ways to get things done. You can serve the clock as automation would serve a machine or you can put time to work for you."[2]

George Shinn has learned how to effectively use time, and it is one of the key reasons for his great success. Shinn is the owner of the NBA basketball team the Charlotte Hornets and operates some thirty other corporations. He believes that "time is a person's most precious commodity."

Shinn says, "The way you occupy your time should be of paramount importance to you. Whatever your goals are, they must be accomplished in the time you have available. Since time is so valuable in achieving your goals, you should consider what robs you of productive time."[3]

Here are some of my suggestions for how to reduce time wasters.

How to Reduce Time Wasters

1. THE LUNCH HOUR: Considering travel and waiting time, a one-hour lunch appointment can easily use up two to three hours of your time. Consider alternatives, such as meeting on the way to/from work for coffee or breakfast or dining in.

2. COMMITTEE MEETINGS: Few activities can waste more time than meetings. Make sure they start on time, end on time, have a definite agenda, and that everyone comes prepared. Maybe even consider having some meetings with everyone standing up.

3. INTERRUPTIONS: When someone walks in, if you are busy, stand up. Your position will automatically reduce the length of the conversation.

> **Power Point**
>
> "To love life is to love time, because time is the stuff that life is made out of."
> —Benjamin Franklin[5]

4. DRIVE TIME: Make your drive time productive by using it to return phone calls (if you are a passenger or can use a phone headset) or listen to teaching/motivational CDs or praise music.

5. IMPROVE YOUR DELEGATING SKILLS: Release activities that can effectively be done by someone else.

Shinn believes that "with forethought and action, you can make your time pay high dividends."[4]

Power Point Question

Which time-wasting activities can you eliminate or drastically reduce?

"It would not be right for us to neglect the ministry of the word of God in order to wait on tables."
—Acts 6:2 (NIV)

Smart money does not jingle

Many vending machines now use wallet-sized plastic cards as a substitute for pocket change.

Reading this article about not needing change for vending machines reminded me of an interesting story I came across years ago. It was about an event that happened to a college vice president who was traveling in South Carolina.

One night, after settling into his motel room, the executive walked down the corridor to where the vending machines were located. He stood looking at a machine trying to decide which item to select.

Just then, a ten-year-old boy walked up, stood beside him, and began to poke quarters into the machine. The boy dropped in three, four, six, eight, ten quarters.

Finally, the executive tapped the boy on the shoulder and said, "Son, son, stop. You're putting way too much money in that machine."

The boy turned to him and proudly said, "Oh no, sir. See, the more money I put in, the more stuff I get out."

A POWERFUL INCREASE PRINCIPLE

This little boy identified one of the key reasons why many achievers do not experience increase in certain areas of their lives: They are not making enough deposits.

For example, I began to experience increased alertness, better stamina, and improved health when I made the decision to increase my deposits of time spent lifting weights and swimming. In the financial arena, when I increased my donations to church and charities, unexpected blessings and unusual business deals were manifested.

The closeness that I enjoy with my children and grandchildren is largely the result of liberal deposits of time in travel, communication, and training.

My spiritual life took on new power and vibrancy when I increased my spiritual deposits. I scheduled regular times of Bible reading, praying, and listening to Scripture-based teaching tapes.

Are you standing next to the vending machine of life wondering why you are not receiving a greater quantity of health, happiness, spiritual endowment, and/or financial rewards? If so, I would suggest that you consider increasing your deposits.

In the words of my friend the late **Dr. Lester Sumrall**, "A person cannot grab their way to success. They release their way to success."

Power Point Question

How might an increase in deposits of time, money, or prayer benefit you?

"The generous soul will be made rich."
—Proverbs 11:25 (NKJV)

Fuss over backward cap

School administrators banned an alumnus from school grounds for six months because he wore a Texas Rangers baseball cap backward.

Because officials considered a backward cap to be possible gang attire, the man had a problem. To overcome the situation with the cap, all he had to do was turn it around.

Likewise, in life, sometimes all we need to do to change a problem into an opportunity is to "turn it around." This is what one of my sons-in-law, **Tim Redmond,** had to do recently.

Tim is a very successful businessman. A little over ten years ago, he played a key role in starting up a computer software company. Under Tim's direction, the business went from four to over four hundred employees. Because of its success, a major national corporation paid millions of dollars to purchase it and its customer base.

Tim took a portion of his proceeds from the sale and made some long-term investments. He then decided to form a company that would conduct success seminars in foreign countries for the purpose of introducing Bible-based success strategies to the audiences.

Because of some contacts that he had in Bolivia, he chose to do his first seminar in the capital city of Santa Cruz. Committing over $25,000 for the program budget, he asked me to join him as a featured speaker. Attendance was expected to be around five hundred.

Ten days before the seminar date, Tim flew to Bolivia for a pre-event inspection trip. He discovered a situation that was disastrous. Although there appeared to be great interest in the seminar, only eighteen people had actually purchased tickets.

TURNING AROUND A "BACKWARD" SITUATION

At this point, most people would probably have cancelled the seminar and taken their losses, but not Tim. Instead, he rolled up his sleeves and, with a fresh determination, he sprang into action.

First he went to the national newspaper and negotiated a trade—ad space in exchange for staff training and free tickets to the seminar. Then he created a group discount program and personally started contacting many local businesses, heralding the benefits of their employees attending the seminar. When I arrived a week later, he had arranged for me to be driven straight to a television station to speak on a national talk show.

> **Power Point**
>
> "When I have eliminated the ways that will not work, I will find the ways that will work."
> —Thomas Edison[2]

By the morning of the seminar, everyone was amazed at the turnaround. In ten days' time, the numbers had skyrocketed from eighteen to over six hundred.

All this happened because one person of vision would not accept it when things were "backward." Instead, he believed enough in himself—and his God—to turn the circumstances around. As Tim says, "Don't be captivated by the height of the mountain rather than your ability to climb."[1]

Power Point Question

What is your instinctive response to negative situations—flight or fight?

_____

"For the battle is the Lord's, and he will give you into our hands."
—1 Samuel 17:47

Healthy habits reduce heart disease

Studies show that small changes in lifestyle patterns and eating habits can greatly reduce the risk of heart disease.

You've heard it before: For better health, eat right and exercise. Millions of people suffer unnecessarily with poor health and die prematurely because they have unhealthy lifestyles, are not eating a proper diet, and are not exercising.

For instance, researchers at the American Heart Association's annual meeting in Atlanta reported that there is more evidence than ever that simple good habits can reduce the risk of heart disease.[1]

Dr. Chris Enriquez, who operates a famous wellness clinic in Ft. Lauderdale, Florida, concurs, "Instead of the traditional reactive approach to health that is so common, I suggest a proactive approach. In other words, I advocate seeking to maintain good health instead of simply reacting whenever bad health comes along."[2]

My friend **Dr. Patrick Quillin**, who is one of America's foremost nutritionists, health lecturers, and broadcasters, also agrees. He states, "Through years of neglect, many people turn their bodies that are built for activity into bodies that can barely get off the couch. Then when their malnourished and poorly maintained bodies begin to break down, they use drugs to subdue the symptoms of the illness, rather than dealing with the underlying cause of the disease."[3]

Dr. Quillin believes that people's lives can change when they come to the realization that "God's purpose for providing food is to nourish the body with essential nutrients found in plants and animals." He states, "You cannot enjoy life as God intended nor accomplish your 'mission' if your body wears out too soon."[4]

From one of his lectures, here are some of Dr. Quillin's ABCs of better health.

ABCs of Better Health

A. ANTIOXIDANTS: Curtail aging and prevent disease by eating plenty of fresh whole fruits and vegetables.

B. BACK MAINTENANCE: The spinal cord is an extension of the brain. Keep it aligned and strong.

C. CHEW FOOD THOROUGHLY: When food is swallowed too quickly, it cannot be absorbed into the body.

D. DRINK FLUIDS BETWEEN MEALS: Drink minimal amounts of fluids while you are eating. They dilute digestive juices. Drink water between meals.

E. E VITAMIN: Several studies have shown that taking vitamin E on a regular basis can reduce the risk of heart attacks.

> **Power Point**
>
> "Our way of life is related to our way of death."
> —Dr. Patrick Quillin[5]

F. FAT REDUCTION: A high-fat diet brings many health hazards, such as clogging of the arteries and acceleration of the aging process.

G. GREEN FOODS: Eat lots of vegetables, some of which should be uncooked. Buy organic produce when possible.

According to Dr. Quillin, we must either take time for wellness or we will be forced to take time for illness.

Power Point Question

Describe what you are doing nutritionally to improve your health.

"Eat what is good and delight yourself with rich nourishment."
—Isaiah 55:2 (author's paraphrase)

Ditchdigger creates canal

The man who extended the Great Northern Railroad through the Rockies constructed a gigantic ditch—the Panama Canal.

History's largest construction project since the building of the great pyramids in Egypt is a "ditch" that goes from one continent to the other. For the builder, **John Stevens**, and his team to set their hands to such a large undertaking required faith and courage.

Hundreds of years ago, faith and courage were also required by the great army of Israel as they faced a crisis. They were about to perish from lack of water. The prophet Elisha instructed them to dig ditches! Against all reason, the soldiers set their hands to a seemingly ridiculous task. However, because of their actions, the Lord brought them deliverance—in the form of water. (See 2 Kings 3:16–20.)

As I read and pondered this story, I wondered, *If God was able to miraculously bring water to the desert, was He not also able to carve out ditches? Why did He tell the Israelites to dig ditches before He brought water?* For me, the answers reveal how God often works.

STEPS TO RECEIVING FROM GOD

1. OBEDIENCE: We will obey God only as much as we trust Him. My friend **John Bevere** says, "When you choose obedience, you choose to fulfill your destiny."[1] Do you trust God enough to do the unexpected? What risks are you willing to take?

2. ACTION: When God is going to show up in a big way, He normally requires us to do something! When we show ourselves strong in faith by our actions, God shows Himself strong through miracles.

This was true throughout the Bible: The widow woman had to get her neighbors' pots, the leper had to dip in the river, and David had to gather five smooth stones.

3. PREPARATION: Through preparation, we can position ourselves to receive the miraculous. Many times, the greater our preparation, the greater the miracle. This concept reminds me of the oft-quoted definition of success given by **Zig Ziglar**: "Success occurs when opportunity meets preparation."[2]

4. PATIENCE: God's work is often an unfolding process. Many times, we will need to wait for the manifestation after we have done what we believe. Our patience is perfected through this waiting and through trusting God, knowing that He will work on our behalf through a divine order and process.

> **Power Point**
>
> "Once you have come to believe God, you demonstrate your faith by what you do."
> —Henry Blackaby[4]

Noted authors **Henry T. Blackaby** and **Claude V. King** write, "This major turning point is where many people miss out on experiencing God's mighty power working through them. If they cannot see exactly how everything can be done, they will not proceed....To follow God, you will have to walk by faith, and faith always requires action."[3]

If you need to dig a ditch or get out of a ditch, start by doing something. Then believe for God to manifest Himself.

Power Point Question

What are you doing to proactively prepare for God's action in your life?

_____

"The soul of the diligent [person] shall be made rich."
—Proverbs 13:4 (NKJV)

Newsboys band takes arena with them

On tour the group sets up their own inflatable, self-contained air dome.

The Newsboys performed concerts in sixty-five cities in the United States during their tour. Their air dome is equipped with a million watts of lighting and 150,000 watts of sound, enough to match most any fixed arena in the country.

This group has been popular for over fifteen years. They have over twenty number-one hits and three gold albums and have sold over three million records.

One of the key reasons that they continue to attract large audiences is that they seek out new and better ways to present their music. While staying consistent in their overall message to music fans of all ages, they periodically reinvent themselves.

UNDERSTANDING YOUR AUDIENCE

In their book, *Shine*, the Newsboys share about the need to keep abreast of one's audience. They believe that the landscape of the world keeps changing. If someone refuses to accept that reality, it causes them to approach the world as they think it should be, rather than as it actually is. The group believes that if we do not learn the way the world thinks and lives, we won't be able to address the real needs of people.[1]

The Newsboys are, in effect, using a selling method called "psychographics." Years ago, I effectively employed it when I was a Chrysler dealer in Southern California. Psychographics is the study and understanding of various segments of the population and their distinct buying habits based upon their values, attitudes, and lifestyles (VALS). After ascertaining the clients' (audiences') value systems, the sales presentation (message, product, or program offering) can be customized based upon this knowledge.

Frank Bettger, who wrote one of the classic books on sales success, teaches this strategy: "Looking back over my career, the biggest regret that I have is that I did not spend twice as much time studying and servicing my customers' interests."[2]

Business consultant and author **Anne Obarski** concurs. She believes that once you know the people you are addressing, you can better provide them with attention-getting communication and products.

Obarski teaches that "people like to do business with people who do not take them for granted."[3] She recommends asking yourself four vital questions. These questions can be adapted for any form of interaction, whether it is for sales, everyday conversation, public speaking, or writing:

- Who are your potential customers?
- Where do they live, work, and play?
- What are the demographics of your typical customers?
- What will attract them and/or bring them back to your company?[4]

Once you really know the audience that you are addressing, you will be better able to furnish the products, services, and programs that best satisfiy their needs and desires.

Power Point Question

How well do you know the needs and wants of your audience or clients?

"Do to others as you would have them do to you."
—Luke 6:31 (NIV)

Tiger Woods wants fair play

Tiger says some new clubs using precision machined, exotic metals should be outlawed, like a corked bat in baseball.

Tiger Woods has been on a rampage, but it hasn't been on the golf course. His tirade comes over huge high-tech drivers obliterating distance records and closing the gap between the merely good and truly great.

Separating the good from the truly great in golf may or may not have to do with the kind of equipment used. However, I am convinced of one thing: Whether or not someone will become truly great in life will depend on how he or she plays the game.

Author **David Curry** has written a book comparing succeeding on the golf course to using principles of the Bible in order to have success in life. He says, "The majority of the Bible is 'principles for living,' not commandments. These principles are ideals and ideas that are applicable in every circumstance of life."[1]

Curry also says, "Golf is infinitely more fun when you are playing the fairway....When I go golfing, I am usually required to bring a three-day ration of food, just in case I get lost. Well, it might not be that bad, but there is a big difference in my level of fulfillment when I am in the fairway as opposed to the rough....In real life, many people like to think of themselves as creative and daring because they live life on the edge. Everything in life is a challenge for these people. They want to do it their way....That is not creativity—that is chaos."[2]

Anyone knows that golf is infinitely easier to play on the fairway than in the rough. The same is true with life. The following are some of David Curry's strategies for living life in the fairway:

Living Life in the Fairway

1. KINDNESS: Kindness is the manner in which we treat people. Instead of being cynical and short, we should be welcoming and gracious.

2. FAITHFULNESS: The world is full of flaky people. You can't count on them to keep their word. Be a person who can be counted on.

3. GENTLENESS: In this rough-and-tumble world, people can be bullied, but we are called to be gentle with others.

4. SELF-CONTROL: Controlling what we say is one of the hardest jobs of all! But we have control over our lives because all things are possible through the power of God.[3]

> Power Point
>
> "The best possible shot is not always to hit the ball directly at the pin."
> —David Curry[4]

The next time you are on the fairway, why not see how many of these Bible-based principles you can use. You may even find yourself adding to the list.

Power Point Question

Are you living life in the "fairway"? Which of the Life in the Fairway principles do you think you need to work on?

"The fruit of the Spirit is love, joy, peace, longsuffering, kindness, goodness, faithfulness, gentleness, self-control."
—Galatians 5:22–23 (NKJV)

Hotels face lawsuits on surcharges

Lawyers are suing corporations that have been billing customers with hidden surcharges for everything from electricity to pool usage.

There are times, such as in the above story, when, in order to settle a grievance, a lawsuit might be necessary. In our society, it is very easy to sue if you believe you have been wronged. However, being the instigator of a lawsuit can have negative consequences such as lost time and money.

For instance, a former Ohio State University football player sued a fellow player for $2 million, claiming that he had punched him. The trial took two weeks. The player spent thousands of dollars for expert witnesses and attorney fees. In the end, he was awarded only $6,000.[1]

Sometimes, the real question to ask is not "Can I?" but rather "Should I?"

TO SUE OR NOT TO SUE

1. ALTERNATE COURSES OF ACTION: Has every other option been examined? Might there be someone, whom both parties respect, who could be a mediator or "communication bridge builder"?

2. OPPOSING PERSPECTIVE: Can you see the issue from the other party's point of view and understand his position and feelings? If he is operating with wrong information and/or wrong beliefs, a meeting or phone call might avoid the cost and time of a suit.

3. CERTAINTY OF OUTCOME: Have you carefully weighed the strengths and legal options of the other side? You could spend a lot of time

and money and then end up with an unfavorable outcome. Also, if the other party countersues, you could end up losing more.

4. ATTENTION DEFICIT: What is pursuing the suit going to cost you, your employees, and/or your company in lost focus and energy? Could you generate more money by spending the same amount of time on increasing income?

5. EMOTIONAL IMPACT: Will pursuing the suit cause you and/or some of your key people to be consumed for a season with negative issues that could trigger personal anger, strife, and hostility? Might this also negatively affect the health, marriages, personal relationships, and/or spiritual power of those involved?

> **Power Point**
>
> "Every problem can be the seed of opportunity for a greater benefit."
> —Deepak Chopra

6. COLLECTING ON THE JUDGMENT: If you win a judgment, but the loser either doesn't have any money or assets or has "buried them," what good is the verdict? Might additional time, money, and effort need to be spent attempting to collect?

7. FORGIVENESS: Have you considered making the matter a "seed" for future harvests? Deepak Chopra teaches that "every problem can be the seed of opportunity for a greater benefit."[2] The apostle Paul in the Bible also taught on this principle: *"Whatsoever a man soweth, that shall he also reap"* (Galatians 6:7).

Before entering into a lawsuit, consider the above points. It could save you a lot of money, headaches, and heartaches.

Power Point Question

Before pursuing a lawsuit, which of the above points should you most consider?

"There is a way that seems right...but in the end it leads to death."
—Proverbs 14:12 (NIV)

Man forgets wife at gas station

A Texas man drove with his wife from Dallas to Oklahoma City. Upon arriving, he was informed by relatives that he had driven off and left her at a highway service station.

I never left my wife behind. However, there was a time when I almost had to fly off and leave my eleven-year-old daughter Michelle behind at one of the world's busiest airports. Instead, we both learned a life lesson that day about the power of spoken words.

"DADDY, I STILL BELIEVE..."

When my children were younger, if I had a weekend speaking trip, I made it a habit, whenever possible, to take one of them with me. Little Michelle was so looking forward to her turn to take her next trip and have Daddy all to herself.

When we arrived at our gate at Los Angeles International Airport, I was faced with a dilemma. The plane was oversold. I had a confirmed assigned seat, but the agent said there was no seat for my daughter. Plus, there were fifteen other standby passengers who had higher priority.

I quickly went over to the gates of the two other airlines that flew to San Francisco. All their flights were sold out. Then I raced back to my gate and tried begging the agent for a seat for my daughter. He again informed me there were no seats. Furthermore, the agent stated that unless I immediately boarded the flight, he was going to give my seat to someone else.

There seemed to be no way for Michelle to come. I quickly got down on my knees and told her that there was not a seat. Mommy would have to take her home. Tears started to roll down her cheeks as she said, "Daddy, I still believe I'll get on that plane."

I tried of think of what words I could say to preserve her precious faith. Just then, the gate agent frantically waved to me. As I rushed over to him, he whispered, "I have one empty seat. Take your daughter with you on the plane." Little Michelle quickly and happily boarded the plane and nestled into the first row, where she was pampered by the attendants the entire flight.

After my speaking engagement, we had a wonderful time together in San Francisco riding the cable cars, going to Fisherman's Wharf, and enjoying the sights.

One other thing: When I sat down in my seat, the man next to me exclaimed, "My wife did not get on the plane. She was out there confessing to me, 'There are too many standbys. I will never get on that plane.'"

As an achiever, it is critical that you realize that great good and change can take place by speaking faith-filled words into negative situations. Train yourself to speak of desired dreams and results.

Power Point Question

Do the words of your mouth create opportunities?

—————————————

"Death and life are in the power of the tongue."
—Proverbs 18:21

Robber steals money from Salvation Army kettle

A gun-toting robber startled shoppers when he ran off with a red kettle that was being used by the Salvation Army for collecting donations.

The Red Kettle fundraising drive, which takes place during the holiday season, raises money to buy toys for needy children and to help the homeless. People were shocked that anyone would steal money intended to help others in need.

Conversely, the lives of my friends **Don and Marlene Ostrom** were changed when they gave money to—not took money from—a charity.

Don and Marlene are multimillionaires who operate eight assisted-living facilities in the Northwest, employing a staff of over four hundred people. Don has traveled to over sixty countries, speaking and teaching people to believe in, and act upon, many of the success principles found in the Bible. He recently came out with a great book called *Millionaire in the Pew*.

Several years ago, Don and Marlene were struggling financially. They had opened one of their first nursing homes. It was a huge 4-story, 140-bed facility. However, they had a problem. There were too many empty beds, and they couldn't seem to get them occupied. As a result, month after month, the facility was running in the red with expenses exceeding income. Sometimes, they had to borrow from other accounts just to cover payroll for that facility. Knowing that the negative situation could not go on much longer, Don was unsure of what to do to turn things around.

One day, Marlene said to him, "Donald, we should give God a donation from this facility." Don exploded, "How can we give from a business that is in the red? We can't give when we aren't making any money! You just don't understand business."

In spite of his logical reasoning, Marlene still felt strongly that they should make a donation. She prayed about the situation. A few weeks later, Don himself felt impressed to do something.

From the facility's account, they made a donation to their church in the amount of one thousand dollars. Don says that "everything changed when we released that money. Almost immediately, the beds began to fill up. Soon, the facility became profitable."[1]

> Power Point
>
> "Everything changed when we released that money."
> —Don Ostrom

Don believes that "the decision to obey God, no matter what the circumstances, established an important core value in my life. It has stayed with me all these years and has brought me exceptional success."[2]

Rabbi Daniel Lapin teaches on the strategy that the Ostroms used to create their financial breakthrough. "How does one go about excavating a money pipeline? Sometimes the only way to get something in is to first dig a route out." He goes on, "Pump money outward from you to the world out there. That action will create conduits that...are able to be used for cash flow in the reverse direction."[3]

As Don says, "God can multiply your obedience many times beyond what you can imagine."

Power Point Question

Might something you release cause you to experience a breakthrough?

_____

"Cast thy bread upon the waters: for thou shalt find it after many days."
—Ecclesiastes 11:1

Thieves steal family history

A lifetime of pictures and videos of the family were among some of the items taken from a couple's station wagon as it sat in their driveway.

The pictures were packed in the vehicle for a trip the next morning to a family reunion. They were the family's only pictures of the children growing up.

Every day, thefts and disasters of different kinds and magnitudes unexpectedly occur. Because of this reality, it is important to focus on protecting your valuable keepsakes and proprietary resources.

This is not to encourage the adoption of a mentality that continually expects bad things to happen. However, it is always best to be aware of possible negative occurrences and to develop prevention and response strategies. In this way, any negative impact will be minimized if and when a harmful situation occurs.

This type of thinking is one reason why former New York City mayor **Rudolph Giuliani** and his officials were able to quickly respond to the tragic events of September 11, 2001. Giuliani shares, "Throughout my time as mayor, we conducted tabletop exercises designed to rehearse our response to a wide variety of contingencies...such as an attack."[1]

You probably will never have to deal with a big disaster. However, a smaller crisis, such as fire or theft, is a distinct possibility. Here are some of my suggestions for how to be disaster resilient.

HOW TO BE DISASTER RESILIENT

1. THINK BACKUP: Back up important documents and computer files regularly. Keep them stored in a safe place off the premises.

2. PROTECT FROM FIRE: Store important pictures, legal documents, and working papers in fireproof cabinets on the premises.

3. LOCK THEM UP: Keep confidential financial and personal material double locked (locked in files in a locked office). Require distinct individual security codes for office entry after hours.

4. PROTECT PRIVACY: Require all employees to sign proprietary rights statements protecting the confidentiality and privacy of customers.

5. ESTABLISH A RECYCLE POLICY: Do not release new confidential information to employees without the old information having been returned.

6. KEEP IT CONFIDENTIAL: Most trash is public domain once it leaves the premises. Place shredding machines in the offices where confidential reports and documents are discarded.

Remember, catastrophic events may be harmful, but they need not be disastrous.

> **Power Point**
>
> "Relentless preparation involves not just preparing for disasters but anticipating potential trouble."
> —Rudolph Guiliani[2]

Power Point Question

Have you adequately protected important pictures, documents, lists, records, and assets?

"Guard what has been entrusted to your care."
—1 Timothy 6:20 (NIV)

Mother battles gator to save son

A twelve-year-old boy who was snorkeling in a river was bitten on the head by the alligator.

Seeing the emergency, the boy's mother reached out and yanked her son from the mouth of the eleven-foot alligator. The ensuing struggle broke the child's leg but saved his life.

In times of emergency, many people somehow receive the courage and ability to do what is seemingly impossible. However, in the normal course of life, if something seems too difficult for them or when they are confronted with what seems impossible, they either don't try or they give up.

Impossibility thinkers are usually passive. They let things happen to them rather than choosing to direct their lives. In addition, new situations frighten them, so they are normally resistant to change.

Author **Dr. Robert Anthony** teaches that this does not need to be our reaction to difficulties because "impossible situations are really only problems for which we have no immediate solution." He believes that "impossible problems are merely the difference between where you are, and where you can be."[1]

For example, up until the turn of the century, flight was considered impossible. Then, one December day in 1903, the Wright brothers succeeded in getting a plane in the air. Suddenly, what was believed to be impossible was possible. In fact, many of the things that we use on a regular basis, such as electric lights, telephones, televisions, microwaves, and personal computers, were all thought to be impossibilities at one time.

CALLED TO DO THE IMPOSSIBLE

Author **Cherie Carter-Scott** says, "Ordinary people believe only in the possible. On the other hand, extraordinary people think about and visualize what is impossible as being possible. By this process they begin to see those things as possible."[2] This was the mind-set that the great industrialist Henry Ford once stated he desired in his employees: "I am looking for a lot of men who have an infinite capacity to not know what can't be done."[3]

The late **Bill Bright** was the founder and president of an international ministry that had a staff of approximately seven thousand people in nearly one hundred countries. He was a man who believed in doing things that seemed to be impossible. In his book *Believing God for the Impossible*, he exhorted his readers, "We are called to do impossible deeds—to live supernatural lives. To live a supernatural lifestyle we must begin to think supernatural thoughts, make supernatural plans, pray for supernatural results, and expect God to work supernaturally in our own lives."[4]

> **Power Point**
>
> "To be a realist, you must believe in miracles."
> —David Ben-Gurion

Anthony Robbins concurs: "People can do virtually anything as long as they muster the resources to believe they can and then take effective action. When you tell yourself you can do it, you open up the pathways that will provide you the resources for achievement."[5] Carter-Scott says, "Whether you believe you can do something or you believe you cannot, you are probably right."[6]

Determine today that the word *impossible* is no longer going to be a barrier to your actions and dreams.

Power Point Question

How can you become a better possibility thinker?

_____

"With God all things are possible."
—Matthew 19:26

747s collide on runway

The worst air disaster in aviation history claims 582 lives at Tenerife Airport.

A s a passenger on the Pam Am 747, **Norm Williams** was en route to a vacation cruise in the Mediterranean. He had no idea that his life would forever be changed in a few tragic moments.

The plane had been flying for several hours when the flight was diverted to an alternate airport. After being delayed several hours, the 747 began to taxi down the airport's single runway. Through the dense fog that had engulfed the airport, their terrified pilot saw fast-approaching lights on the runway in front of him. Panic gripped him as he realized that it was another plane taking off toward them on the same runway.

The pilot screamed on the radio, "We're on the runway." The other jet, a KLM 747, lifted up sharply from the runway. It almost cleared the Pan Am 747. However, its landing gear ripped off the top of the plane's fuselage, sending it toppling on its side.[1]

Norm exclaimed, "There was instant fire, explosions, screams, falling ceilings, and havoc. People who were only inches apart were suddenly separated, one to life and one to death. However, in the midst of all that was happening, I sensed the presence of God. I felt like I was programmed to survive. Even though I was a part of the tragedy, I was separated from fear, insulated from death."[2]

I was with Norm at a meeting in California where he shared what happened next. He looked up and noticed that there was a large gash in the cabin ceiling revealing the sky above. He knew that it would be impossible for him to lift his 6-foot, 250-pound frame some 10 feet and then grab the ragged edges of that blasted fuselage. How it happened, he does not know—but he did it. He then jumped thirty feet from the oily wing to the ground below. Having injured his ankle from the fall, he hurriedly hobbled away from the burning plane. Hearing a loud ground-shaking explosion, he jerked himself around and saw the plane disappear in a flaming inferno.

In the Bible, there is a story of three men, Shadrach, Meshach, and Abednego, who faced a threat similar to Norm Williams'. At the king's order, they were thrown into a fiery furnace. Daniel 3:27 states, *"The princes, governors, and captains...saw these men, upon whose bodies the fire had no power."* Afterward, the king stated that he believed God had saved them from death by sending an angel to deliver them because they *"trusted in him"* (verse 28).

> **Power Point**
>
> "I felt like I was programmed to survive."
> —Norm Williams

Norm believes that his life was spared because, for years, he had spent time reading and meditating on the Bible's teachings on divine protection.

Power Point Question

Are the protection Scriptures of the Bible imbedded in your subconscious?

"I will be with thee...when thou walkest through the fire."
—Isaiah 43:2

Governor forgets tuxedo

Thirty minutes before a formal dinner with the president at the White House, the governor discovered that he had left his tuxedo back home.

In spite of the above dilemma, the governor was able to attend the function properly dressed. His wife, who was decked out in a beautiful new dress for the festive occasion, quickly thought of a solution. She hustled her husband down to the hotel kitchen. There she was able to locate a waiter's tuxedo. That night, the governor took a ribbing from those who learned of his fate. They kept asking him for more coffee.

The governor knew that it would be improper to attend a formal dinner such as this without a tuxedo. Protocol required certain attire. The same is true for you in the marketplace of life.

Frank Bettger, in his classic book on sales success, *How I Raised Myself from Failure to Success in Selling*, says, "Clothes do not make a man, but they do make 90 percent of what you see of him."[1] Unless someone looks the part, people will not believe that what he or she says is important. So here is the most practical idea that I have ever heard on how to improve your appearance: "Put yourself in the hands of an expert."[2]

John Molloy is such a person. He is "America's First Wardrobe Engineer," and his books on attire, such as *Dress for Success*, are classics. He says, "People who possess wealth...do set themselves apart by distinctive patterns of speech and dress. People who look successful receive preferential treatment in almost all of their social and business encounters."[3]

Years ago, I had an opportunity to put his theory to a test. It occurred at Houston Airport, where I had boarded a flight to Cancun, Mexico. Having come from a speaking engagement, I arrived at the airport wearing a suit and tie. I went to a restroom and, for my flight to the resort destination, changed into jeans and a casual shirt. After I had waited on the plane for an hour, they announced that the plane had mechanical problems and that the flight was being cancelled. People flocked out of the plane and rushed to the agent at the gate. Although the agent was apologetic about the situation, the airline was not offering to put the stranded passengers up for the night or compensate them for the inconvenience.

> **Power Point**
>
> "People who look successful receive preferential treatment."
> —John Molloy

After listening to him refuse to do anything for several other passengers, other than to rebook them on a flight the next day, I sprang into action. I went back into the restroom and put on the clothes that I had worn to the airport—my "power outfit," a dark blue suit with a white shirt and silk tie. When my turn came to converse with the agent, his attitude toward me was totally different. He gave me a meal voucher for dinner and issued me a coupon for a free night at the airport Marriott.

Molloy also believes that "successful dress cannot put a boob in the boardroom, but incorrect dress can definitely keep an intelligent man out."[4]

Power Point Question

How could a better awareness of your attire cause increase in your life?

_____

"He...changed his raiment, and came in unto Pharaoh."
—Genesis 41:14

New movie features 10-minute segments

In a new twist at moviemaking, fifteen different film directors were given exactly 10 minutes to present their story and vision on screen.

No one can get more time, but we all can do a better job utilizing the time we have." So states my good friend **Sharon Cook**, who is a seminar teacher, event planner, and musical producer. Sharon teaches people how to reduce stress while becoming more productive.

One of her strategies for increasing personal productivity is to become more aware of, and better utilize, the numerous 10-minute segments of time that make up each day.

Sharon reminds us that "there are six 10-minute segments in every hour, one hundred forty-four 10-minute segments in every day, and one thousand eight 10-minute segments in every week. The choices we make as to how we value and use these 10-minute segments has a lot to do with personal productivity and happiness in life."

10-MINUTE CHOICES

Sharon illustrates how one can change circumstances in this short period of time: "By spending 10 minutes in quiet meditation, one can totally switch one's reaction to stress and busyness. Napping for 10 minutes can release fresh energy and clearer thinking. Within 10 minutes, a mother can stop what she is doing, bandage her crying toddler's scraped knee, plant a kiss on the child's forehead, and within 10 minutes be perceived as 'Mother of the Year.' Likewise, a husband can come home after having had an earlier disagreement with his wife, bring her flowers, say the words 'I'm sorry,' and, within 10 minutes, change the course of the whole evening and maybe even their future."

In the spiritual area of life, capturing these short time segments can make a difference. "Spending 10 minutes a day in prayer can bring you joy and make you more peaceable. God can touch your broken spirit and take away your grief or doubt. In that 10 minutes, you begin to believe that all things are possible. In 10 minutes, you can come forth from a dead situation; spiritual eyes can be opened, and you can get the understanding and creative ideas needed for a turnaround. Spending 10 minutes a day reading the Bible can add new power and authority to your life. Additionally, teaching Bible stories and principles to your children or grandchildren for 10 minutes a day can give them a foundation for greater success and a life of purpose."

> ### Power Point
>
> "Unless time is managed, nothing else can be managed."
> —Peter Drucker[1]

Of course, Sharon does not believe that everything in one's life will be fixed in 10 minutes. Some things will take patience and perseverance. However, she does believe that "within 10 minutes, one can receive the wisdom and insight to know what to do and how to fix it."

Sharon says, "If you do not manage your time, it will manage you, so start doing that now—10 minutes at a time."

Power Point Question

How can you better utilize your 10-minute segments of time?

"To every thing there is a...time."
—Ecclesiastes 3:1

Chef fired for good cooking

A Swedish cook was fired because his cooking was so good that it was creating lines and causing a shortage of tables.

The restaurant manager told reporters that the cook was terminated because "he was attracting too many people."

This article reminded me of an experience that I had a few years ago in the Palm Springs area of California. Based upon some friends' recommendations, I visited a fast-food restaurant called In-N-Out Burgers for the first time.

The store was located along the interstate adjacent to two other nationally renowned fast-food outlets. As I arrived, I was surprised at the difference in the number of cars in the parking lots and drive-thru lines of the three establishments. One restaurant had three vehicles, the next one had six vehicles, and In-N-Out Burgers had thirty-one vehicles. That's right—over 500 percent more vehicles!

I became excited about going inside to discover what would cause this great difference in customer numbers. The restaurant was sparkling clean, but I knew it had to be more than that. The menu offered only six items, so I knew it sure wasn't that. As I sat down and began to eat one of the best hamburgers I have ever enjoyed, I saw the answers. They were right in front of me—written on my place mat.

There I read the following: "At In-N-Out Burgers, we've always believed that freshness makes a difference you can taste: Our hamburgers are made from fresh, 100 percent pure, locally raised American beef. We make every In-N-Out burger one at a time, cooked fresh to your order. Our buns are baked using old-fashioned sponge dough and contain no preservatives. We don't own a single freezer, microwave, or heat lamp. We make our french fries from real potatoes—fresh each day. Our shakes are still made from real ice cream instead of artificial shake mix." And the list of unique characteristics went on and on.

Success guru and best-selling author **Tom Peters** believes that "for the successful company, quality cannot just be one more competitive weapon—it must be a consuming passion." He also believes that "quality is perceptual and subjective. It is delivering above expectation. It is having products that contain a 'delight factor'... a startling little touch that makes a customer smile."[1]

> ### Power Point
>
> "Quality...must be a consuming passion."
> —Tom Peters

If you don't mind dealing with problems caused by having too many customers or too much income, then take time today to ponder these questions: What are you offering compared to your competition? How can you become the best? The people are out there waiting for you.

Power Point Question

How can you create greater uniqueness for your products and/or services?

"And a great multitude...followed him...when they had heard what great things he did."
—Mark 3:7–8

Prayer makes a difference

Ruth Graham is now home and well after teetering on the brink of death for five days.

When her fever, brought on by spinal meningitis, reached 104 degrees, her husband prayed for a miracle. **Billy Graham** believed that prayer would help his wife, **Ruth**, to recover. Shortly after he prayed, she sat up in bed, asked the nurses for ice cream, and then pleaded to go home.

Rev. Graham and other people in ministry are not alone in their belief that prayer can change natural circumstances. In a survey conducted by the American Academy of Family Physicians, virtually all the doctors questioned believed in a link between the spirit and the health of their patients.[1]

Other recent scientific studies support this view.

In the first known study linking religious faith and prayer to heart patient recovery, a public hospital in San Francisco took four hundred heart patients and divided them into two groups. In the double-blind study, one group was prayed for by strangers who received their names, while the other group was not prayed for. The group that was not prayed for suffered congestive heart failure two and a half times more than the group that was prayed for.[2]

In another study, Dartmouth Medical School tracked 232 open-heart surgery patients for six months. They found that "the patients who received no strength or comfort from religious faith were over three times (300 percent) more likely to die."[3]

Charles Stanley, a renowned author, pastor, and national television personality, says, "For a long time the deity of [God] was nothing more to me than Orthodox theology. That is, until I began to think about the fact that God's Spirit dwells in me."[4] Charles then came to the realization that the presence of God can enable anyone to live a life of greater victory over circumstances.

The late **Norman Vincent Peale** greatly believed in the power of prayer. He said, "The flow of power between the creator and man is the world's greatest power. I know what prayer has done for me, and over and over again I have seen what it can do for others."[5]

Robert Schuller agrees. He states, "The greatest power in the world today is the power of people to communicate with Almighty God."[6]

Noted authors **Henry T. Blackaby** and **Claude V. King** say that, after you pray, you need to do one more thing: "Immediately anticipate the activity of God in answer to your prayers. Expect Him to answer."[7]

> **Power Point**
>
> "The greatest gift you can give anybody is to pray on their behalf."
> —George W. Bush[8]

Billy Graham believes that, when he prayed for his wife, power was released that brought healing into her body. Through prayer, you also have this force available to you. It is the power to overcome adversity and to change the course of natural events.

Power Point Question

How can you better activate the power of prayer?

———————————

"[We] *should always pray and not give up."*
—Luke 18:1 (NIV)

Over one million cars stolen

The Insurance Information Institute reports that in America over one million cars are stolen each year. That is one car every twenty-three seconds.

When **Alexander Berardi's** car was stolen, he did not care about the other million or so vehicles that were stolen that year. For him, it was the day that the "bottom fell out."

As a young man, Alex went through a desperate season in his life. After his dad died, he floundered aimlessly. He graduated from high school and then began working three jobs—one full-time and two part-time. Yet a recession was raging, and companies everywhere started laying off workers by the thousands. Alex became one of those statistics.

Two weeks after he lost his high-paying factory job, his apartment was burglarized. Because all his furniture was stolen, he was forced to sleep on the floor. Two months went by. His part-time jobs barely gave him enough money for food, and his cash was running out. His mother used her connections to get him a job working as an orderly at a local hospital. But the job was at night, and it, also, was only part-time.

His minimum-wage jobs did not provide enough money to cover his expenses. Soon, his landlord asked him to make other living arrangements. That was when he moved into his car. It was a ten-year-old forest green Ford Thunderbird, with three hubcaps, bald tires, and bad brakes—but it was home.

Things were bad, but early one morning a few weeks later, Alex would reach the lowest point of his young life.

He says, "I stood staring emotionless at the empty parking space where, only hours earlier, at the beginning of the night shift, I had left my car. Exhausted, I collapsed onto the curb. My world was ripping apart at the seams as I sat in the gutter, cold, hungry, retching, and writhing in pain from a sickening migraine headache. And now, I was homeless with nothing left but the clothes on my back."

TURNING FAILURE INTO SUCCESS

For the next several months, Alex lived on the streets. He did so while trying to maintain a status-quo image at work because not too many employers want to keep a "bum" on their payroll. He discovered that he was far more resilient than he had realized and was capable of overcoming far more than he ever thought possible.

That understanding, plus the tenacity that he developed during those months, helped him to bounce back and become successful in business. Today, he speaks and motivates audiences around the world. His book, *Never Offer Your Comb to a Bald Man*, has sold over a million copies.

> **Power Point**
>
> "Even one's failures are successes! They represent the miracle that we survived."
> —T. D. Jakes[3]

Alex says that if we live long enough, we will all experience our share of the good, the bad, and the ugly.[1] The object is not just to go through these experiences but to grow through them.[2]

Power Point Question

Do you create learning experiences out of hard times?

"All things work together for good to them that love God, [and]...are the called according to his purpose."
—Romans 8:28

Man gives 30 gallons of blood

According to the Red Cross, during his lifetime, an Oklahoma man has given over 30 gallons of blood.

In 1951, wanting to do something to help his fellowmen, **Bennie Willmann** came up with the idea of donating his blood. Since blood can be donated only one pint at a time, he has made over 240 visits to the blood center.

Bennie says that he is just an ordinary man, a former Marine who fought during World War II. He exclaims, "Not being rich, I had to give what I could. What more could someone do than to help give life to another person?"

I salute Bennie for his compassion and commitment to helping others. He has the right priorities and is doing positive and inspiring things with his life.

To me, this is a good example of what a person's life should be based upon: reaching beyond one's own world to be a blessing to others.

What if more people, who were also financially successful, had the same value system and compassion as Bennie? In a lifetime, what kind of positive impact could their lives have on others?

As a reader of this book, you already have determined to achieve greater success. Why not achieve it based upon a life of giving and helping others? What greater purpose could you possess than to be a blessing to those in need?

Not only will your life have an impact on others, but you will also be happier and more fulfilled. Psychologist **William James** stated, "The only truly happy people that I have ever known are those who have found a cause greater than themselves to live for."[1]

Having this perspective gives living a fresh meaning. It releases within you excitement and a new inner power that directs and propels your days.

In addition, you will be more blessed. Throughout the Bible, God brought increase to those who were willing to release what they had to help others. To be this kind of person, it will require you to personally redefine your meaning of success. For you, success must be measured not only by what you get and/or accumulate but also by what you give.

Create your own "power points." Let them be the places and times where you have an opportunity to release blessings into other people's lives.

As **Ted Turner** says (who has given hundreds of millions of dollars to charities), "Regardless of how busy we get in our daily lives, we must take time out to identify areas and ways in which we can help others."[2]

> **Power Point**
>
> "Don't live beyond your means; give beyond your means."
> —Rabbi Daniel Lapin[4]

It might be giving clothes to charities or taking food to needy families. Maybe it is forming the habit of tipping at drive-thru windows and/or becoming a monthly donor to charities that are helping hurting people.

On the other hand, for you it could be setting a goal to give at least $100,000 per year to your church or synagogue. Maybe it is donating a million dollars to a cause that you deeply believe in.

Whatever you can do, begin now. One of the greatest givers of all time, **Bill Gates**, says, "The dream is not about getting rich but about making a difference."[3]

Power Point Question

What actions can you take this week to positively impact others?

"A generous man devises generous things, and by generosity he shall stand."
—Isaiah 32:8

Endnotes

Power Point #1: Turtle falls from sky

[1] Denis Waitley, *Timing Is Everything* (Nashville: Thomas Nelson Publishers, 1992), 6–7.

Power Point #2: Wrong house raided

[1] Rudolph Giuliani, *Leadership* (New York: Hyperion, 2002), 122.

[2] Donald Trump, *Trump: The Art of the Deal* (New York: Warner Books, 1987), 52.

Power Point #4: Giant sinkhole swallows home

[1] Gary Smalley, *Hidden Keys of a Loving, Lasting Marriage* (Grand Rapids, Michigan: Zondervan Publishing House, 1988), 18–19.

[2] Ibid., 332.

[3] Ibid., 18–19.

Power Point #5: Giuliani starts investment firm

[1] Rudolph Giuliani, *Leadership* (New York: Hyperion, 2002), 117.

[2] Ibid., 43.

[3] Ibid., xi–xii.

[4] Ibid., xii.

Power Point #6: Barry Bonds joins 700 club

[1] Anthony Robbins, *Unlimited Power* (New York: Fawcett Columbine, 1986), 230–231.

Power Point #7: Teen riding waves after shark attack

[1] "Girl Who Lost Arm to Shark Surfs in Meet," The Associated Press, posted on Herald.com, 11 January 2004. <http://www.miami.com/mld/miamiherald/sports/7682153.htm> (14 January 20, 2004)

[2] Jill Lieber, "Teen Riding Wave of Amazing Grace," *USA Today,* 19 March 2004, 15C.

[3] Ibid.

[4] <http://www.topicsites.com/booker-t-washtington/booker-t-washington-quotes.htm>

Power Point #8: Zig Ziglar receives award

[1] *Get Motivated Workbook* (Tampa, Florida: Peter Lowe Seminars, 2003), 18, and <http://www.ziglartraining.com/Ziglar/zigziglar.do> (22 January 2004)

[2] <www.quotationspage.com/search.php3?Author=Zig+Ziglar&file=other> (November 17, 2004)

Power Point #9: Government has eye that never sleeps

[1] T. D. Jakes, *Loose That Man and Let Him Go* (Tulsa: Albury Press, 1995), 93.

[2] Laurie Beth Jones, *Jesus-Led* (New York: Hyperion, 1996), 22.

[3] Author's quote archives; source unknown.

[4] Richard Exley, *The Rhythm of Life* (Tulsa: Honor Books, 1987), 60.

[5] Donald Trump, *Trump: Surviving at the Top* (New York: Random House, 1990), 114.

Power Point #10: New York cabbie sick after check bounces

[1] John Chapin, ed., *The Book of Catholic Quotations* (New York: Farrar, Straus and Cudahy, 1956), 724.

Power Point #11: Survival attitude helps downed pilot

[1] Bruce, B. Auster, "One Amazing Kid," *U.S. News and World Report,* June 19, 1995. <http://www.f-16.net/library/stories/ogrady.html> (12 January 2004)

[2] Dexter Yager, speech, Gooch Free Enterprise Weekend, Knoxville, Tennessee, September 1990.

Power Point #13: Resort town bans ties

[1] JohnnyCarson,<http://www.brainyquote.com/quotes/quotes/j/johnnycars158444.html>

[2] Joe Gibbs, *Game Plans for Success* (Boston: Little, Brown, and Company, 1995), 155.

[3] Zig Ziglar, July 1990 Success Seminar, Honolulu, Hawaii.

[4] Joe Griffith, *Speaker's Library of Business Stories* (Englewood Cliffs, N.J.: Prentice Hall, 1990,) 266–67.

[6] Ibid.

Power Point #14: Collision with pole restores eyesight

1 Jerome Edmondson, *Maximizing Misfortune* (Shippensburg, Pennsylvania: Treasure House, 2003), 53.

2 Ibid., 56.

Power Point #15: American swimmers told not to spit in pool

1 Van Crouch, *Winning 101: Insight and Motivation to Help You Achieve Excellence* (Tulsa: Honor Books, 1995), 108.

2 Personal conversation, St. Louis, Missouri, October 1999.

Power Point #16: Man searches for his father

1 Dr. James Dobson, *Straight Talk* (Dallas: Word Publishing, 1991), 62.

2 Lee Iacocca, *Talking Straight,* (New York: Bantam Books, 1988), 24.

3 *God's Little Devotional Book for Dads* (Tulsa: Honor Books, 1995), 219.

4 Lee Iacocca, *Talking Straight,* 23.

5 Ibid, 24.

Power Point #17: Doctors warned about exploding patients

1 Tim LaHaye, *Anger Is a Choice* (Grand Rapids: Zondervan, 1982), 156.

2 Derek Prince, *God's Remedy for Rejection* (New Kensington, PA: Whitaker House, 1993) 70–71.

3 LaHaye, *Anger Is a Choice*, 156.

Power Point #18: Star is rich and lonely

1 Dr. Patrick Quillin, *Healing Secrets from the Bible* (Canton, Ohio: The Leader Company, 1995), 21.

2 Catherine Marshall, *To Live Again* (New York: Fawcett World Library, 1970), 42.

3 Ibid., 45.

4 Ibid., 42.

Power Point #19: Swimmer loses trunks during race

1 Paul G. Stoltz, *Adversity Quotient: Turning Obstacles into Opportunities* (New York: John Wiley & Sons, 1997), 67.

2 Anthony Robbins, *Unlimited Power* (New York: Fawcett Columbine, 1987), 198.

3 <http://www.usatennisflorida.usta.com/news/fullstory.sps?iNewsID=51348 &itype=1107&iCategoryID=>

Power Point #20: Fish removed from man's nose
[1] Les Brown, *Live Your Dreams* (New York: William Morrow and Company, 1992), 41.
[2] Ibid., 49.

Power Point #21: Cadillac crashes into bedroom
[1] Lewis Lord, *U.S. News and World Report,* 6 December 1999, 76.
[2] <http://www.pbs.org/wgbh/amex/quizshow/sfeature/part5.html>
[3] Dr. Joyce Brothers, *The Successful Woman* (New York: Simon and Schuster, 1988), 49.
[4] Ibid.
[5] Alvin Toffler from *Powershift: Knowledge, Wealth, and Violence at the Edge of the 21st Century*, 2, 1990, quoted in Leonard Roy Frank, ed., *Random House Webster's Quotionary* (New York: Random House, 2001), 430.
[6] Harvey McKay, *Beware the Naked Man Who Offers You His Shirt* (New York: Ivy Books, 1990), 78.

Power Point #22: Governor Schwarzenegger announces recovery plan
[1] <http://www.uk-lerning.net/t20288.html>
[2] Leo Rosten, *Leo Rosten's Treasury of Jewish Quotations* (New York: McGraw-Hill Book Company/The Jewish Publication Society of America, 1972), 182.

Power Point #23: Blind man robs bank, then cannot find way out
[1] Leo Rosten, *Leo Rosten's Treasury of Jewish Quotations* (New York: McGraw-Hill Book Company/The Jewish Publication Society of America, 1972), 233.

Power Point #24: Stocks ignoring bad economic news
[1] Lou Tice, *Smart Talk for Achieving Your Potential* (Seattle, Washington: Pacific Institute Publishing, 1995), 59.
[2] Ibid., 62.

Power Point #25: Joe Gibbs rejoins Redskins
[1] Ray Didinger, *Game Plans* (Boston: Little, Brown, and Company, 1995), 39.

Power Point #26: 92-year-old woman gets 30-year mortgage
[1] John Mason, *An Enemy Called Average* (Tulsa: Harrison House, 1990), 52.

Power Point #27: Man hit by lightning on golf course

[1] Personal conversation with author, Indianapolis, Indiana, October 1997.

[2] Zig Ziglar, *Top Performance* (New York: Berkley Books, 1987), 43.

[3] TV Special, Tulsa Community College, channel 21, Tulsa, Oklahoma, 15 March 2002.

[4] Norman Vincent Peale, *Bible Power for Successful Living* (New York: Peale Center for Christian Living, 1993), 130.

Power Point #28: Man comes out of coma

[1] Personal conversation with author.

Power Point #29: Toilet paper theft causes firing

[1] J. C. Watts, *Decision* magazine, July 2004, 15.

Power Point #30: Car falls seven floors

[1] Robert Schuller, *Power Thoughts* (New York: Harper-Collins Publishers, 1993), 21.

[2] <http://www.crystalcathedral.org/about/aboutrhs.html> (20 January 2004)

[3] Robert Schuller, *Power Thoughts* (New York: Harper-Collins Publishers, 1995), 92.

[4] Ibid.

[5] Robert Schuller, *Power Thoughts* (1993), 67.

Power Point #31: Families left out in the cold

[1] Rabbi Daniel Lapin, *Thou Shall Prosper* (Hoboken, New York: John Wiley and Sons, 2002), 19.

Power Point #32: Government feeds and cares for monkeys

[1] For a discussion of this topic, please refer to Kenneth Blanchard, William Oncken, Jr., and Hal Burrows, *The One-Minute Manager Meets the Monkey* (New York: Quill William Morrow, 1989).

[2] Ibid.

Power Point #34: Quarterback leaves Pro Bowl early

[1] Anthony Robbins, *Unlimited Power* (New York: Fawcett Columbine, 1986), 298.

Power Point #35: With low-cal movement, less is more
[1] Laurie Beth Jones, *Jesus-CEO* (New York: Hyperion Press, 1955), 77.

Power Point #36: Palm Desert buys university
[1] <http://www.thinkarete.com/quotes/by_teacher/abraham_lincoln> (August 16, 2004)

Power Point #37: Bugging devices cause political furor
[1] *Business Travel News,* June 1995.
[2] Charles R. Smith, "Big Brother on Board," newsmax.com, 11 December 2003. <http://www.newsmax.com/archives/articles/2003/12/10/213653.shtml> (August 13, 2004)
[3] Ibid.
[4] *Meeting News,* 8 April 2004, 1.

Power Point #38: Parents made kids eat rats and roaches
[1] Robert H. Schuller, *Self-Esteem: The New Reformation* (Waco: Word Books, 1982), 34.
[2] Zig Ziglar, *Top Performance* (New York: Berkley Books, 1986), 91.
[3] Colin Powell, personal conversation with author, Indianapolis, 1997.

Power Point #39: New lease on life
[1] Edna Harrison-Harlin, *A Second Chance at Love* (Garden Grove, CA: New Lease Publishers, 1984), 60.

Power Point #40: Man hugs tree to escape fine
[1] Dewey Freidel, *Real Men Wear Boxer Shorts* (Shippensburg, Pennsylvania: Destiny Image Publishers, 1995), 139.
[2] <http://www.cellularmemory.net/PEC.htm>
[3] Dewey Freidel, *Real Men,* 139.
[4] *USA Today,* 11 January 2001, 1D.
[5] Jack Canfield and Mark Victor Hansen, *Dare to Win,* (Newport Beach, California: self-published, 1988), 90.

Power Point #42: Dead woman sheds a tear
[1] http://www.brainyquote.com/quotes/authors/r/robert_collier.html(December 22, 2004)

Power Point #43: Last Oldsmobile rolls off line

[1] Leonard Ray Frank, *Random House Webster's Quotionary* (New York: Random House, 2001), 759.

Power Point #44: Governor says "thanks" to firms

[1] Joe Griffith, *Speaker's Library of Business Stories* (Englewood Cliffs, New Jersey: Prentice Hall, 1990), 266.

[2] Zig Ziglar, *Top Performance* (New York: Berkley Books, 1986), 178.

[3] Richard Capen, Jr., *Finish Strong* (San Francisco: Harper/Zondervan, 1996), 81.

[4] *The Power Newsletter* (Amway), March 1996, 7.

[5] Wanda Loskot, SanMarketing.com. <http://www.sanemarketing.com/articles/tank.html> (November 5, 2004)

Power Point #45: Charity gets moving in new van

[1] Anthony Robbins, *Unlimited Power* (New York: Fawcett Columbine, 1986), 220.

[2] Tom Hopkins, *How to Master the Art of Selling,* (Scottsdale, Arizona: Tom Hopkins International, 1982), 93.

Power Point #46: Cruise ship runs aground

[1] Gavin and Patti MacLeod, *Back on Course* (Old Tappen, New Jersey: Fleming H. Revell Company, 1987), 93.

[2] Ibid., 140.

Power Point #47: City starts automated trash removal

[1] Joe Griffith, *Speaker's Library of Business Stories* (Englewood Cliffs, New Jersey: Prentice Hall, 1990), 356.

[2] Ronnie Belanger and Brian Mast, eds., *Profiles of Success* (North Brunswick, New Jersey: Bridge-Logos Publishing, 1999), 160.

[3] Ibid., 59.

[4] Author's quote archives; source unknown.

Power Point #48: Graham awarded Congressional Medal

[1] "Billy Graham," *Tulsa World,* 9 May 1996, A16 (Editorial).

[2] Vernon McLellan, *Billy Graham: A Tribute from Friends* (Colorado Springs, Colorado: Warner Books, 2002), 25.

[3] Billy Graham, *Just As I Am* (Carmel, New York: Guideposts [by special arrangement with HarperSan Francisco Publishers], 1997), 128.

[4] Ibid.

[5] Edwin Louis Cole, *Courage: A Book for Champions* (Tulsa: Honor Books, 1985), 90.

[6] John Wooden, *They Call Me Coach* (Waco, Texas: Word Books, 1985).

[7] <http://www.brainyquote.com/quotes/authors/b/billy_graham.html> (10 May 2004)

Power Point #49: Asian elephant born in captivity

[1] Myles Munroe, *The Principles and Power of Vision* (New Kensington: Whitaker House, 2003), 99.

[2] Ibid., 217.

[3] Ibid., 103.

[4] Lee Iacocca, *Iacocca—An Autobiography* (New York: Bantam Books, 1984), 281.

[5] Bill Gates, "Technology," *Price-Costco Connection,* December 1996, 43.

Power Point #50: Woman rides out tornado in bathtub

[1] Tom Landry, *An Autobiography—Tom Landry* (New York: Harper Paperbacks, 1990), 286.

Power Point #51: Family disappears on the road to nowhere

[1] Stephen R. Covey, *The Seven Habits of Highly Effective People* (New York: Simon and Schuster, 1989), 99.

[2] <http://www.motivatingquotes.com/goalsq.htm> (December 23, 2004)

[3] Covey, *Seven Habits,* 97.

[4] Ibid., 98.

Power Point #52: Cities finding gold in parking fees and fines

[1] *Travel Weekly,* June 1995, 12.

Power Point #53: Nails removed from man's head

[1] John Maxwell, *Attitude 101* (Nashville: Thomas Nelson Publishers, 2003), 11.

[2] Ibid., 12.

[3] Ibid., 5.

Power Point #57: Can found inside of fish

1 Les Brown, *Live Your Dreams* (New York: William Morrow and Company, 1992), 211.

Power Point #59: Student jailed for udder nonsense

1 Anthony Robbins, *Unlimited Power* (New York: Fawcett Columbine, 1986), 220.

Power Point #60: McDonald's heiress fills buckets

1 Richard Exley, *The Rhythm of Life* (Tulsa: Honor Books, 1987), 108.
2 David Whelan, "In the World of the Wealthy, Who Gives?" Forbes.com, 28 September 2004. <http://www.msnbc.msn.com/id/6123392> (October 3, 2004)
3 John Templeton, *Discovering the Laws of Life* (New York: Continuum Publishing, 1994), 298.
4 Jill Lieber, "The Sport of Giving," *USA Today*, 26 December 2003, C1.
5 Ibid.
6 Ibid.
7 Ginnie Graham, "Don't Look Now, But Rick Couri's Going Fishing for a Good Cause," *Tulsa World,* 10 May 2004, A1, and "$40,660 Raised by Zingo Rider," *Tulsa World,* 21 June 1990, A22.
8 Richard Exley, *The Rhythm of Life*, 108.
9 Lieber, "The Sport of Giving," C1.
10 Templeton, *Laws of Life,* 299.

Power Point #61: Vegetarians becoming flexitarians

1 <http://en.proverbia.net/citasautor.asp?nombre=George+Bernard&apellidos =Shaw&autor=16652&page=9> (December 2, 2004)
2 <http://www.brainyquote.com/quotes/authors/h/henry_ford.html> (December 2, 2004)
3 <http://www.zaadz.com/quotes/authors/john_h_patterson/> (August 9, 2004)
4 Jacquelyn Wonder and Priscilla Donovan, *The Flexibility Factor* (Ballantine Books, 1991), 6.

Power Point #62: Doorman refuses to hail cab

1 <http://www.cnn.com/HEALTH/library/EP/00002.html> (October 27, 2004)

[2] "It's Never Too Late to Start Living a Healthier Lifestyle," *Prime Life Styles*. <http://www.goerie.com/primelifestyles/it_s_never_too_late_to_start_ 1.html> (August 9, 2004)

[3] Kenneth W. Cooper, *Aerobics* (New York: Bantam Books, 1968), 24.

[4] Ibid., inside cover of book jacket.

[5] <http://www.cnn.com/HEALTH/library/EP/00002.html> (October 27, 2004)

Power Point #63: Bill to scrap inspections is ok'd

[1] Robert Nelson, quoted in *Skills for Success* (Bristol, Vermont: The Soundview Executive Book Summaries, 1989), 90.

[2] John Maxwell, *Developing the Leader within You* (Nashville: Nelson Books, 1993), 28.

[3] David Ingles, personal conversation with author, June 1999.

[4] *Skills for Success,* 89.

[5] Joyce Meyer, meeting at Mabee Center, Tulsa, Oklahoma, June 2003.

Power Point #64: Dead woman gets job back

[1] Arvella Schuller, *The Positive Family* (Garden City, NJ: Doubleday-Galilee, 1982), 31.

[2] Jan Stoop and Betty Southward, *The Grandmother Book* (Nashville: Thomas Nelson Publishers, 1993), 135.

[3] Ibid., 38.

[4] Arvella Schuller, *The Positive Family,* 21.

Power Point #65: Saboteurs derail train

[1] Stephen Covey, *First Things First* (New York: Simon and Schuster, 1994), 36.

[2] Stephen Covey, *The Seven Habits of Highly Effective People* (New York: Simon and Schuster, 1989), 148.

Power Point #67: Globe littered with land mines

[1] John R. Noe, *Peak Performance Principles for High Achievers* (New York: Frederick Fell Publishers, 1984), 96.

[2] Ibid., 41.

[3] Ibid., 96.

[4] The first three "Land Mines of the Past" quotes come from Gemmy Allen, "Supervision," online course, Mountain View College, Dallas, Texas, 1998.

Source: http://ollie.dcccd.edu/mgmt1374/book_contents/2planning/plng_
process/change.htm> (August 24, 2004)

[5] *National Inquirer*, 20 June 2000, 20.

[6] This and the previous quote come from Gemmy Allen, "Supervision" online
course.

[7] *National Inquirer* 20 June 2000, 20.

[8] John R. Noe, *Peak Performance,* 105.

Power Point #68: Contest officials search for God

[1] Stephen R. Covey, *The Seven Habits of Highly Effective People* (New York:
Simon and Schuster, 1989), 277.

[2] Ibid., 284.

[3] Florence Littauer, *Dare to Dream* (Waco, Texas: W Publishing Group, 1991),
12.

Power Point #69: Varmints stink up school

[1] Phillip C. McGraw, *Life Strategies* (New York: Hyperion, 1999), 68.

[2] Phillip C. McGraw, *Self Matters* (New York: Simon and Schuster, 2001),
192.

[3] General Norman Schwarzkopf, personal conversation, St Louis, Missouri.

[4] John Mason, Hawaii Increase Event, March 1995.

[5] Mark Victor Hansen, IBI Seminar, Long Beach, California, November 1994.

[6] Dexter Yager, *Don't Let Anybody Steal Your Dreams* (Charlotte, NC: Internet
Services, 1993), 31.

[7] Charles Swindoll, *Living Above the Level of Mediocrity* (Waco Texas: Word
Books, 1987), 81.

[8] Colin Powell, personal conversation with author, Indiana, October 1997.

[9] *Ministries Today,* March 1999, 24.

Power Point #70: Chick-fil-A wins quality award

[1] <http://www.chick-fil-a.com>

[2] See also S. Truett Cathy, *It Is Easier to Succeed Than to Fail* (Nashville:
Thomas Nelson Publishers, 1989), 16.

[3] Robert Schuller, *Power Thoughts* (New York: Harper-Collins, 1993), 65.

[4] Ibid., 37.

[5] Myles Munroe, *The Principles and Power of Vision* (New Kensington:
Whitaker House, 2003), 198.

[6] Schuller, *Power Thoughts,* 142.

[7] S. Truett Cathy, *It is Easier to Succeed,* 13.

Power Point #71: 200,000 paid for lunch

[1] <www.nyse.com/press/1022834145706.html> (27 August 2004)=

[2] <www.pbs.org/wgbh/pages/frontline/shows/scandal/inside/cron.html> (27 August 2004)

Power Point #72: Many still in the dark

[1] *Tulsa World,* 17 June 2004, A-12.

[2] Myles Munroe, *The Principles and Power of Vision* (New Kensington: Whitaker House, 2003), 11.

[3] Ibid., 11–12.

[4] Ibid., 13.

[5] Ibid., 32.

[6] James Stovall, *You Don't Have to be Blind to See* (Nashville: Thomas Nelson Publishers, 1996), 2.

Power Point #73: Elevator suddenly plunges

[1] Tom Peters, *Thriving on Chaos* (New York: Harper-Perennial, 1987), 108.

Power Point #74: Ugly lamp brings small fortune

[1] Paul G. Stoltz, *Adversity Quotient: Turning Obstacles into Opportunities* (New York: John Wiley & Sons, 1997), 66.

[2] Jim Collins, *Good to Great* (New York: Harper Business, 2001), 13.

Power Point #75: Movie star makes deathbed confessions

[1] Stephen R. Covey, *The Seven Habits of Highly Effective People* (New York: Simon and Schuster, 1989), 97.

Power Point #76: Student honesty linked to discounts

[1] Joe Griffith, *Speaker's Library of Business Stories* (Englewood Cliffs, New Jersey: Prentice Hall, 1990), 152.

[2] Ibid.

Power Point #77: Sheriff is resident of jail he built

[1] Lou Tice, *Smart Talk* (Seattle, Washington: Pacific Institute Publishing, 1995), 11.

² Suze Orman, *9 Steps to Financial Freedom* (New York: Crown Publishers, 1997), 7.

Power Point #78: Bush parachutes for his 80th birthday

¹ Zig Ziglar, *Courtship after Marriage* (Nashville: Thomas Nelson Publishers, 1990), 240.

² Billy Graham during guest appearance on *Larry King Live,* date unknown.

³ Zig Ziglar, *Courtship after Marriage,* 19.

⁴ *Tulsa World,* 8 September 2004, C-6.

⁵ Gary Smalley, *Hidden Keys of a Loving, Lasting Marriage* (Grand Rapids, Michigan: Zondervan Publishing House, 1988), 42.

⁶ Arvella Schuller, *The Positive Family* (Garden City, NJ: Doubleday-Galilee, 1982), 67.

⁷ Randy J. Gibbs, *20/20 Vision* (New York: Daybreak Books, 1998), 96.

Power Point #79: Arab sheik buys 40 college degrees

¹ Les Brown, *Live Your Dreams* (New York: William Morrow and Company, 1992), 49.

Power Point #80: Jet crashes short of runway

¹ Julie Schmit, *USA Today,* 4 April 1995, B1.

² Herbert Freudenberger, *Burn Out* (Garden City, New York: Anchor Press, 1980), 210.

Power Point #81: Wife victimized by chiseling Romeo

¹ See Jim Guinn, "Christian Con Men: The New Breed," *RMAI,* Fall/Winter 1995.

² Myles Munroe, Global Leadership Summit, Nassau, Bahamas, 12 November 2002.

³ Marilyn Hickey, ICBM Conference, Tulsa, Oklahoma, 1 June 2002.

⁴ Ken Blanchard, *The Heart of a Leader* (Tulsa: Honor Books, 1999), 56.

Power Point #82: Bird causes power outage at airport

¹ <http://www.tulsaworld.com/archivesearch/Search/ArchiveArticleConfirm.asp?articleID=362889>

² Jack Canfield, Mark Victor Hansen, and Les Hewitt, *The Power of Focus* (Deerfield Beach, FL: Health Communications, 2000), 173.

[3] Gary Smalley, *Hidden Keys of a Loving, Lasting Marriage* (Grand Rapids, Michigan: Zondervan Publishing House, 1988), 267.

[4] Phillip C. McGraw, *Life Strategies* (New York: Hyperion, 1999), 167.

[5] See Dennis Byrd, *Rise and Walk: The Trials and Triumph of Dennis Byrd* (New York: HarperCollins, 1993).

[6] Phillip C. McGraw, *Life Strategies,* 167.

Power Point #83: Man trapped in outhouse overnight

[1] Dr. Patrick Quillin, "Biblical Health Secrets," Bob Harrison Hawaii Increase Event, March 1999.

[2] Edwin Feldman, *How to Use Your Time to Get Things Done* (New York: Fredrick Fell Publishers, 1968), 62.

[3] George Shinn, *Miracle of Motivation* (Wheaton: Living Books, 1981), 168.

[4] Ibid.

[5] Edwin Feldman, *How to Use Your Time,* 8.

Power Point #85: Fuss over backward cap

[1] Tim Redmond, *Words of Promise* (Tulsa: Honor Books, 1995), 94.

[2] Harvey McKay, *Beware the Naked Man Who Offers You His Shirt* (New York: Ivy Books, 1990), 373.

Power Point #86: Healthy habits reduce heart disease

[1] Linda Ciampa, "Healthy Habits Can Reduce Risk of Heart Disease," CNN, 9 November 1999. <http://www.cnn.com/HEALTH/9911/09/heart.food/> (21 January 2004)

[2] Dr. Chris Enriquez, M.D., *The Healthy Life* (New Kensington: Whitaker House, 2004), 16.

[3] Dr. Patrick Quillin, *Healing Secrets from the Bible* (Canton, Ohio: The Leader Company, 1995), 1.

[4] Ibid., 7.

[5] Ibid., 13.

Power Point #87: Ditchdigger creates canal

[1] Personal conversation with author.

[2] <http://eclaunchsite.com/ECLbusquotes.htm#Z> (September 22, 2004)

[3] Henry T. Blackaby and Claude V. King, *Experiencing God* (Nashville: Broadman & Holman, 1998), 58.

⁴ Henry T. Blackaby and Claude V. King, *Experiencing God*, 233.

Power Point #88: Newsboys band takes arena with them

¹ Newsboys, *Shine* (New Kensington, Pennsylvania: Whitaker House, 2002), 42.

² Frank Bettger, *How I Raised Myself from Failure to Success in Selling* (New York: Simon & Schuster, 1982,) 156.

³ Anne M. Obarski, *Surprising Secrets of Mystery Shoppers: 10 Steps to Quality Service That Keep Customers Coming Back!* (Tarentum, Pennsylvania: Word Association Publishers), 77.

⁴ Ibid., 18–19.

⁵ Tom Peters, *Thriving on Chaos* (New York: Harper-Perennial, 1987), 108.

Power Point #89: Tiger Woods wants fair play

¹ David Curry, *God Plays Golf!* (New Kensington, PA: Whitaker House, 2001, 2003), 37.

² Ibid., 30–31.

³ Ibid., 38–39.

⁴ Ibid, 14.

Power Point #90: Hotels face lawsuits on surcharges

¹ <http://espn.go.com/nfl/news/2003/0430/1547404.html>

² Deepak Chopra, *The Seven Spiritual Laws of Success* (San Rafael, California: Amber-Allen Publishing, 1994), 89.

Power Point #91: Man forgets wife at gas station

¹ Charles Stanley, *The Wonderful Spirit-Filled Life* (Nashville: Thomas Nelson Publishers, 1995), 77.

Power Point #92: Robber steals money from Salvation Army kettle

¹ Don Ostrom, *Millionaire in the Pew* (Tulsa: Insight Publishing Group, 2004), 112.

² Ibid., 90.

³ Rabbi Daniel Lapin, *Thou Shall Prosper* (Hoboken, New York: John Wiley and Sons, 2002), 307.

Power Point #93: Thieves steal family history

¹ Rudolph Giuliani, *Leadership* (New York: Hyperion, 2002), 62.

[2] Ibid., 64.

Power Point #94: Mother battles gator to save son

[1] Dr. Robert Anthony, *How to Make the Impossible Possible* (New York: Berkley Books, 1996), 66.

[2] Cherie Carter-Scott, television interview, 28 May 2003.

[3] <http://www.quotationspage.com/quotes/Henry_Ford> (December 23, 2004)

[4] Bill Bright, *Believing God for the Impossible* (San Bernardino, California: Here's Life Publishers, 1979), 42, 46.

[5] Anthony Robbins, *Unlimited Power* (New York: Fawcett Columbine, 1986), 15.

[6] Cherie Carter-Scott, television interview, 28 May 2003.

Power Point #95: 747s collide on runway

[1] Margot Cleary, *Great Disasters of the Twentieth Century* (New York: Gallery Books, 1990), 90.

[2] Norman Williams, *Terror at Tenerife* (Van Nuys, California: Bible Voices, Inc., 1977), 63, 65.

Power Point #96: Governor forgets tuxedo

[1] Frank Bettger, *How I Raised Myself from Failure to Success in Selling* (New York: Simon & Schuster, 1982), 98.

[2] Ibid.

[3] John Molloy, *Dress for Success* (New York: Peter Wyden Publishers, 1975), 2.

[4] Ibid., 9.

Power Point #97: New movie features 10-minute segments

[1] Joe Griffith, *Speaker's Library of Business Stories* (Englewood Cliffs, N.J.: Prentice Hall, 1990), 355.

Power Point #98: Chef fired for good cooking

[1] Tom Peters, *Thriving on Chaos* (New York: Harper-Perennial, 1987), 102.

Power Point #99: Prayer makes a difference

[1] Dana Sterling, "Praying to Get Well," *Tulsa World,* 19 December 1996, A1–2.

[2] Ibid.

[3] Ibid.

[4] Charles Stanley, *The Wonderful Spirit-filled Life* (Nashville: Thomas Nelson Publishers, 1992), 5.

[5] Norman Vincent Peale, *The Power of the Plus Factor* (Old Tappan, New Jersey: Fleming H Revell, 1987), 122.

[6] Robert Schuller, *Positive Prayers for Power-filled Living* (New York: Hawthorne Books, 1976), inside flap of book jacket.

[7] Henry T. Blackaby and Claude V. King, *Experiencing God* (Nashville: Broadman & Hollman, 1998), 180–81.

[8] Barbara Wheeler, M.D., "America's Prayer Network Newsletter," Washington, D.C., September 2004.

Power Point #100: Over one million cars stolen

[1] Alexander J. Berardi, *Never Offer Your Comb to a Bald Man* (Novato, California: New World Library, 2001), 94.

[2] Ibid., 229.

[3] T. D. Jakes, *Loose That Man and Let Him Go* (Tulsa: Albury Press, 1995), 95.

Power Point #101: Man gives 30 gallons of blood

[1] Richard Exley, *The Rhythm of Life* (Tulsa: Honor Books, 1987), 108.

[2] James Stovel, *Success Secrets of Super Achievers* (Tulsa: Narrative Television Network, 2001), 153.

[3] Bill Gates, "Technology," *Price-Cosco Connection*, December 1996, 43.

[4] Rabbi Daniel Lapin, *Thou Shalt Prosper* (Hoboken, New Jersey: John Wiley and Sons, 2002), 298.

About the Author

Bob Harrison is America's leading increase activist. He is an author, a sales achiever, a business owner, a television personality, and an electrifying speaker.

Harrison teaches corporate and business groups worldwide and is a featured speaker at super achiever seminars costing $5,000 per person. In addition, he teaches at the largest success seminars in America, sharing with audiences of up to 20,000 people.

Known as "Dr. Increase," Harrison speaks from the heart of a man who has lived the gamut of experiences—inspired challenges, near failures, thrilling victories, and astonishing sales success. At one time, he was millions of dollars in debt and on the verge of bankruptcy. In one week's time, he completely turned the situation around and experienced a dramatic breakthrough.

Harrison specializes in teaching on success in marriage and finances. Countless homes and businesses have been transformed and turned around by applying the principles that he dramatically shares. His valuable material has been shared with thousands of businesses, corporations, seminar groups, and television audiences worldwide.

Harrison has a degree in Business Management from California State University. He is president of Harrison International Seminars in Tulsa, Oklahoma.

Now you, too, can benefit from his years of accumulated knowledge and experience combined with a powerful message that produces real financial and personal success.

For additional information on seminars and scheduling speaking engagements, or to contact the author, please direct your correspondence to:

2109 East 69th Street
Tulsa, OK 74136
1-800-632-4653
1-918-496-3399
e-mail: increase@increase.org
website: www.increase.org

*From the pages of the book
comes this dynamic teaching series.*

POWER POINTS
for
SUCCESS

Commentary & Teaching
by Bob Harrison

*With skill, insight, and humor, Bob Harrison shares stories and
gives commentary about the strategies that enable people to rise
from the status quo to a life of excellence and greatness. He
shares proven methods, along with step-by-step directions on
how to appy knowledge in practical, everyday situations. Learn
how you can experience new power, thrilling victories, and great
personal and financial victories in every area of your life.*

Harrison International Seminars
2109 E. 69th St.
Tulsa, OK 74136
800-632-4653; Fax 918-496-3072
www.increase.org

BOB HARRISON
"Dr. Increase"
CD & Tape Seminar Series
Over One Million Tapes & Cds Purchased

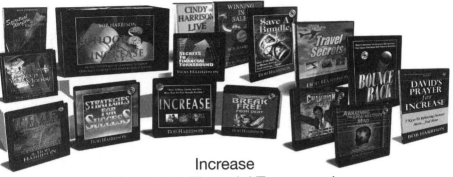

Increase
Secrets to Financial Turnaround
How to Keep Your Money
Break Free Financially
Save A Bundle
Strategies for Success
Time Increase
Awakening the Great Multitude Mind
Big Battles - Big Rewards
Travel Secrets
Spiritual Warfare and Your Money
Winning in Sales
Better Homes and Marriages
Your Marriage Matters
Raising Champion Families
Bounce Back

DVD Series
David's Prayer for Increase

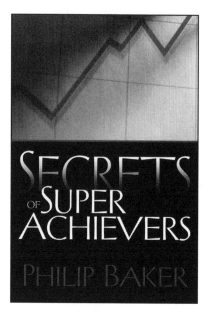

Secrets of Super Achievers
Philip Baker

Have you ever noticed someone who seems to have it all—a great family, financial security, and an adventurous outlook on new challenges? A great life does not happen by accident—it is chosen and requires desire, determination, and faith. Those who refuse to let life happen to them, but instead choose to make life happen, boldly break away from the security of mediocrity and eagerly chase God's best for their lives. Philip Baker provides insight and direction for those seeking to be more than just average and greater than the status quo. He shows readers the secrets to perseverance, balance, focus, endurance, and courage, all with a humor and wisdom that compels and enlightens.

ISBN: 0-88368-806-9 • Hardcover • 192 pages

www.whitakerhouse.com

www.deepercalling.com